Angel María de Lera

Twayne's World Authors Series

Janet Pérez, Editor of Spanish Literature

Texas Tech University

TWAS 652

Angel María de Lera

By Mary Sue Listerman

Miami University

Twayne Publishers • *Boston*

Angel María de Lera

Mary Sue Listerman

Copyright © 1982 by
G. K. Hall & Company
Published by Twayne Publishers
A Division of G. K. Hall & Company
70 Lincoln Street
Boston, Massachusetts 02111

Book Production by John Amburg

Book Design by Barbara Anderson

Printed on permanent/durable acid-free
paper and bound in The United States of
America.

Library of Congress Cataloging in Publication Data

Listerman, Mary Sue, 1940–
  Angel María de Lera.

  (Twayne's world authors series ; TWAS 652)
  Bibliography: p. 146
  Includes index.
  1. Lera, Angel María de, 1912– —Criticism
and interpretation. I. Title. II. Series.
PQ6621.E67Z76   863'.64   81-7192
ISBN 0-8057-6495-X   AACR2

To Randy and Devin

Contents

About the Author

Mary Sue Hanks Listerman was born on April 16, 1940, in Houston, Texas, where she lived until graduation from Lamar High School in 1958. Her B.A. was completed at Southern Methodist University (Dallas, Texas) in 1962, where she majored in elementary education and minored in religion. She received the Ph.D. degree in May 1973 from the University of Missouri at Columbia. She is currently an associate professor of Spanish at Miami University, Ohio, where she has taught for 14 years.

Publications and specialized teaching interests have included the poetry of Juan Ramón Jiménez; the mysticism of Santa Teresa; the drama of Federico García Lorca; and the novels of Angel María de Lera. Subsequent travel experiences have included year residencies in Cologne, Germany and Madrid, a summer residency in Aguadulce, Spain, and visits to Granada, Córdoba, and Sevilla. Her future plans involve the pursuit of a Master of Theology degree.

Preface

Angel María de Lera (b. 1912) fought in the Spanish Civil War on the Republican side, was jailed in 1939, and was sentenced to death. Yet this unusual man, whose own life is novelesque, surmounted not only that obstacle, but innumerable others, to be recognized today as a widely read and respected novelist. Although he arrived late on the literary scene—his first novel, *Los olvidados* [The Forgotten Ones], was published in 1957—one cannot speak of the contemporary Spanish novel without mentioning his name and production.

Los clarines del miedo [The Horns of Fear, 1958] brought him instant fame both at home and abroad, and his subsequent works have enjoyed a rapid diffusion, often heading the best-seller list for months at a time. He has shown an admirable, disciplined energy (having published seventeen works within a twenty-year period), as well as an ability not only to equal, but in some instances to surpass his earlier successes. Proof of the latter is the fact that four of the most important literary prizes of Spain were awarded to some of his later works: the Premio Pérez Galdós and the Premio Alvarez Quintero of the Real Academia for *Tierra para morir* [Land to Die In, 1964]; the coveted Premio Planeta[1] for *Las últimas banderas* [The Last Flags, 1967] which is now in its thirty-third edition;[2] and the Ateneo de Sevilla for *Se vende un hombre* [A Man Sells Himself, 1973].

Notwithstanding the fact that his vision of the Spanish people is neither amiable nor falsely idyllic, he has succeeded in reaching a wide mass of foreign readers. Translations of his novels have been published in Germany, Canada, the United States, Finland, France, Hungary, England, Italy, and Sweden; and four have been adapted for the Spanish screen. In addition to the individual editions of his works, a collection of five appeared in 1965 (from the publishing house of Aguilar, with a prologue by Luis Escolar Bareno), and an abridged edition of *Los clarines del miedo* has been prepared for classroom use.[3]

It is difficult to place a popular writer such as Lera in a literary category, both because of his awkward position chronologically among contemporary novelists and because of his independence of any one school. He is a transitional figure who embodies the classical Spanish heritage in literature, but who, with sometimes prophetic vision, confronts the basic social and political issues of his time. For the material of his novels he relies heavily on his personal experiences: the tetralogy of the Civil War is, for example, largely autobiographical. Furthermore, he is still writing, and more time is needed before his definitive contribution to Hispanic letters can be assessed.

The point of view of this book will be that of the close relationship between the life of the author and his works, as well as the reflection that they present of contemporary Spain from 1936 to the present. Emphasis is placed on the storytelling ability of the author and the unity of form and content. For this reason, and because most readers will not be familiar with his works, I have followed an analysis technique that relates the story in some detail, including literary criticism within this structure.

By means of the arrangement of the novels, I hope to show the progressive pattern of Lera's life and work corresponding to Spain's own progression from internal strife, through the Franco era, to final emergence as a democratic nation incorporated into modern Europe. Due to the page limitations of this volume, I have chosen to discuss only the novels, making reference where applicable to the nonfiction works (designated as such in the Bibliography). Also not included is the author's last published novel (July 1979) entitled *El hombre que volvió del paraíso* [The Man Who Returned from Paradise].

In the summer of 1972, I spent a week in Madrid and was granted a daily interview with Lera. Although he was under some harassment from the Franco government at the time, and unable to publish his war novels, I was able to discuss freely all aspects of his work and to meet and visit with his family. Thus some material in this book will be direct quotations from that interview.

Another source of information for this volume is my doctoral dissertation,[4] the first to be written about the author, for which I read in detail all his then-published works, as well as large amounts of critical material. I have also made limited use of two other completed doctoral disserations: "El desarraigo en las novelas de Angel María de Lera" by Ellen Lismore Leeder (University of Miami, December 1973), and "La novelística de Angel María de Lera" by Gayle Wehr (Florida State University, 1974).[5]

Finally, I would like to give credit to Antonio Heras, whose critical biography of Lera, written in 1971 and entitled *Angel María de Lera*, was helpful to me in the realm of biographical material and stylistics.

Mary Sue Listerman

Miami University

Acknowledgments

I would like to express my appreciation to Professor Albert Brent of the University of Missouri, my dissertation advisor, and to Professor Stanley Payne of Miami University, who gave me encouragement to write this book.

I am indebted to Angel María de Lera for granting me an interview, and to Professor Janet W. Pérez, my editor.

I am grateful for the clerical assistance of Mrs. Eudora Dunkin, Miss Cindy Payne and Miss Linda White.

I am thankful to my family and friends for their support.

Chronology

1912   May 7: born in the village of Baides (Guadalajara).
        Family later moves to Membrilla (Ciudad Real) and then
        Cortijos de Arriba de Fuente el Fresno (Ciudad Real).

1918   Family moves to Lanciego (Alava).

1920   Family moves to Laguardia (Alava).

1923   Enters Seminary of Vitoria to study philosophy and
        humanities and to prepare for the priesthood.

1926   Death of his physician father, Ángel Julio de Lera y
        Buesa, in an epidemic of pneumonia.

1930   Leaves the seminary. Goes to live with his mother, María
        Cristina García Delgado, in Línea de la Concepción
        (Cádiz). (Fall of Dictatorship of Primo de Rivera.)

1931   Receives *bachillerato* from the Instituto del Cardenal
        Cisneros in Madrid. (April 14: Second Republic
        formed.)

1932   Begins to study law at the University of Granada.

1935   Becomes secretary of the Syndicalist party formed by
        Angel Pestaña.

1936   (Outbreak of Spanish Civil War.) Flees to Gibraltar and
        then to Madrid, where he becomes Commissioner of
        War for the Republicans.

1939   (End of Spanish Civil War.) April 21: imprisoned in the
        provisional prison in the Glorieta de San Bernardo y
        Vallehermosa, 7 (Madrid). May 1: condemned to death.
        May 29: sent to prison of San Antón; sentence com-
        muted to thirty years. September: sent to Penal de
        Ocaña; sentence commuted to twelve years. (Outbreak
        of World War II.)

1942   Sent to Penal de Aranjuez.

1943   Sent to Penal de Santa Rita (Madrid).

1944   Provisional liberty from the Prison of Guadalajara.

1946   Returned to Prison of Zaragoza.

1947   Final liberty. Returns to Madrid. He is now thirty-five.

1948   Accountant for small liquor distillery, a position he holds for fourteen years.

1950   Marries María Luisa Menes Martín.

1951   Birth of son, Angel Carlos. Death of mother.

1955   Writes *Los olvidados*.

1956   *Los clarines del miedo* is finalist in the Premio Nadal.

1957   *Los olvidados* published. Writes *Bronce* (or *La Juerga*), which is never published.

1958   *Los clarines del miedo*. Birth of daughter Adelaida.

1959   *La boda*. Movie version of *Los clarines del miedo* at Cine Rialto.

1960   *Bochorno*.

1962   *Trampa*. Assignment to Germany for *ABC*.

1963   *Hemos perdido el sol*. Movie version of *Bochorno* at Cine Rialto. Writes series for *ABC* on the Spanish emigrant workers in Germany.

1964   *Tierra para morir* published and receives two literary awards: Pérez Galdós and Alvarez Quintero (of the Real Academia).

1965   *Con la maleta al hombro*. Movie version of *La boda* at Cine Torre. Collected *Novelas* published by Aguilar.

1966   *Por los caminos de la medicina rural*.

1967   *Las últimas banderas* published and wins the Premio Planeta.

1968   *Los fanáticos*. Begins to write *Los que perdimos*.

1969   Lecture tour of sixteen American universities (USA).

1971   Elected president of the Mutualidad de Escritores. Finishes *Los que perdimos*.

1972 *Mi viaje alrededor de la locura.*

1973 *Se vende un hombre.*

1974 *Los que perdimos.*

1976 (Death of Francisco Franco. Reestablishment of Monarchy under Juan Carlos.) *La noche sin riberas.*

1977 *Oscuro amanecer* published. (Adolfo Suárez elected Prime Minister on June 15.)

1978 *Angel Pestaña.* (New Constitution ratified.)

Chapter One
Life and Times
Childhood and Adolescence

Angel María de Lera (b. 1912) was born in Baides, province of Guadalajara. His father, Angel Julio de Lera y Buesa, was a rural doctor whose humanitarian qualities and early death in 1925 left a lasting impression on the author. Memories of Lera's father are reflected in several of the novels, particularly in the figure of the doctor Jesús in *Los olvidados* [The Forgotten Ones]. Lera's mother, María García Delgado, survived the Civil War but died of Parkinson's disease in 1951. The couple had four sons and four daughters:[1] only Lera himself and two of his sisters (Adelaida and María Guillermina) are living today.

Because of his father's profession, the family lived in various villages of Ciudad Real, la Mancha, and la Rioja. As Luis Escolar Bareno observes, these rural roots "would be decisive in the personality and literary works of Lera. The hard manchega landscape . . . its primitive people, somber, at times to the point of sordidness, yet profound and human, will form the peasant background of celtiberic roughness that we discover in some of his novels. The Rioja, rough, but of a more varied and abrupt landscape, with more receptivity for the simple pleasures of life, will [also] be reflected in the personality of Lera."[2]

At the age of eleven, Lera entered the ecclesiastical seminary of Vitoria, where he studied humanities and philosophy before abandoning his religious career at the age of eighteen. In Spain, traditionally Catholic, this decision to withdraw from preparation for the priesthood speaks loudly of the valiant and decisive character of Lera, who preferred religious and social censorship rather than to remain in that profession without a true calling.

In 1930 he moved to la Línea de la Concepción (Cádiz) to live with his widowed mother and two sisters. This date coincided with the fall of the dictatorship of Primo de Rivera and the subsequent establishment of the Second Republic in 1931. During these years he was politically active, associating himself with the Anarchist-Syndicalist Movement under the leadership of Angel Pestaña, and becoming Secretary General of the party. (Pestaña, the hero of his youth, is the subject of a recent biography by Lera.)[3] He also completed his *bachillerato* (high-school equivalent) at the Instituto del Cardenal Cisneros in Madrid, and initiated law studies at the University of Granada. The Spanish Civil War broke out, however, in 1936, only a few months prior to his final examinations.

Civil War and Prison

When the war began, Lera was in Nationalist territory but escaped to Gibraltar, and later found himself in Madrid as Commissioner of War for the Republicans. There he participated in the historic last days of the conflict (1939) and the subsequent surrender of the Republican forces to General Franco. These experiences are novelized in *Las últimas banderas* [The Last Flags], the first of his war tetralogy; the remaining three novels are related to his years as a political prisoner.

Arrested on April 21, 1939, Lera entered the provisional prison of the Glorieta de San Bernardo y Vallehermosa (Madrid), where he was interrogated and sentenced to death on May 1. He was then transferred to the prison of San Antón, where his sentence was commuted to thirty years. The second novel of the tetralogy, *Los que perdimos* [We Who Lost], corresponds to those first months. Then in September he was transferred to the prison of Ocaña, where he spent more than three years, as is depicted in *Noche sin riberas* [Night without Shores]. During 1942 and 1943, the height of World War II, he was confined in the prisons of Aranjuez and Santa Rita (Madrid), respectively, and in 1944 was granted provisional liberty from the prison of Guadalajara, only to be returned to Zaragoza prison in 1946. His final release came in 1947, at which time he returned to a hostile postwar Madrid, bearing the stigma of "war criminal." These latter trials complete the tetralogy in the novel entitled *Oscuro amanecer* [Dark Dawn].

Understandably, the war years and subsequent imprisonment were decisive in the author's life, encompassing as they did, his young adulthood. The tetralogy of novels was written later over a twelve-year period (1966–1978), enabling the author not only to achieve the necessary balance and perspective, but to work through the painful memories of those experiences. This self-purging, necessary for himself, is representative of the large amount of Civil War literature published over the past fifteen years that has helped the country to stabilize itself and to heal old wounds.[4] Lera's courage was shown, not only in choosing to remain in Spain when many intellectuals had fled, but also in publishing his novels there (the last two were released only after the death of Franco).

New Beginnings

As pointed out in the Preface, there is a close unity between the author and his works, as well as with the slow emergence of Spain from the trauma of civil conflict. The years in prison, corresponding to the oppression under Franco, are followed by the fight for survival in economically depressed postwar Spain. It is a progression that reflects an evolution from the microcosm to the macrocosm, a continual building on the past echoing the theme of the emergence of consciousness or identity which is present in all of the novels. Eduardo de Guzmán comments that "in the years subsequent to the revealing of his first novel, Angel María de Lera continues an uninterrupted, ascending spiral. In constant personal improvement, each one of his published stories has greater ambition and transcendence than the preceding one, and in all of them he addresses with resolution and accuracy the current problems of contemporary Spain. In each new work he poses questions that encompass wider sectors and that are able to penetrate more deeply into the present and future of [Spain]."[5]

Lera began life again at age thirty-five with nothing but his own existence. He held a variety of jobs from street peddler to construction worker and insurance salesman before finding stable employment in 1947 as an accountant in a small distillery on the outskirts of Madrid. He retained this position for fourteen years, aided by the support and friendship of his employer Manuel Vega Sierra.

During those years he married María Luisa Menes Martín (in 1950) and rejoiced in the birth of a son, Angel Carlos, in 1951. Until 1955, Lera's struggle for survival left him no time to write (he had married with a salary of 1,200 *pesetas* monthly, which was only twenty dollars). He began his novelistic career using a pencil, writing on old invoices from the distillery. Later during mealtimes, he would "borrow" the office typewriter to make a clear draft. Thus in 1957 at age forty-five, he produced his first novel, *Los olvidados* [The Forgotten Ones], a description of the misery in a slum area which Lera crossed on his way to and from work. These humble beginnings on the road to fulfillment led to the next stage of the expanding spiral of his life, a search for roots or a usable past, which he found in the Spanish villages of his childhood. It was an emotionally intense period for the writer, a reflection of the vitality and tension of a man for whom, indeed, life began at forty. Further inspired by the birth of a daughter, Adelaida, the result is two works of great contention and force.

Los clarines del miedo [The Horns of Fear, 1958] is set in a small village of la Mancha, dealing with the traditional theme of the bullfight, but viewed from an original perspective, and strongly intermeshed with the peoples of that region. *La boda* [The Wedding, 1959] also has a rural setting and delves deeply into the cultural and psychological roots of the nation. Lera's own fear and continuing struggle against hunger and a repressive society are echoed in the novels, but there is a stronger note of hope, perhaps related to his budding recognition from the reading public.

Bochorno [Summer Storm, 1960] and *Trampa* [The Trap, 1962] attempt to broaden the author's sphere of experience and influence. Focusing on the capital of Madrid as representative of modern Spanish society, they treat of the middle and upper classes, respectively. Lera was by then the bourgeois head of a family with a steady job, and had moved to a small apartment in the Calle de Londres (where he currently resides). Although in a sense a dream realized, this life was somewhat at odds with the personality and adventurous spirit of Lera. As a result, there is a lack of vitality and a heaviness, too readily seen in the figure of the father Luis in *Bochorno,* a middle-class "morality play" condemning modern day materialism. Likewise, his treatment of the upper class in *Trampa* is limited by conflicting attitudes: in this instance, class prejudice and a lack of familiarity with the environment and the theme of homosexuality, which he tries to develop.

Not long after, however, the author became professionally independent, determining to live off the royalties of his novels, and aided by his admittance into the world of journalism. His articles were printed by the leading newspapers and journals of Spain (particularly the Madrid daily *ABC*), where he gave voice to his numerous social and intellectual concerns. According to Eduardo de Guzmán, writing in the Prologue to *Los fanáticos* (a collection of Lera's articles), "[he] is already a magnificent journalist . . . almost daily he displays his clear journalistic sense . . . an example and model of modern journalism. . . . He deals with an extraordinary variety of themes, treated always with sincerity of expression and profundity of thought. Generally they are not trivial or intranscendental [themes]; even when the original event that he comments upon may be so. The writer knows how to elevate himself, apparently without effort, to transform the particular into the general and to arrive at conclusions which are as accurate as they are logical."[6] A self-educated man, Lera read assiduously, and for some years had been given access to the personal library of the cinema writer Antonio Vich. As Lera's biographer Antonio Heras relates: "Antonio Vich confessed to me that he has never been able to understand how Angel was capable of reading such a quantity of pages in such a short time. He [had] a real necessity to read . . . an ardent desire to improve himself."[7]

New Horizons

Lera's adventurous and ever-curious spirits were allowed a new breath when in 1962 he received a special assignment from *ABC* that enabled him to tour numerous cities in Germany for the purpose of interviewing the Spanish emigrants working there. The articles written for *ABC* were later expanded and published under the title *Con la maleta al hombro* [With My Knapsack on My Shoulder, 1965], and this preoccupation with emigration, one of the most important socioeconomic problems of his country, found further expression in the novel *Hemos perdido el sol* [We Have Lost the Sun, 1963].

This widening of horizons from a vantage point outside Spain caused the questioning of old values, resulting in a recognition of the need for adaptability and change, as well as international cooperation. These ideas are reflected in a novel about the abandoned villages in Spain, *Tierra para morir* [Land to Die In, 1964]. Thus, as is his method, Lera progresses on his road, but always brings his new knowledge and experience to bear on the needs and problems of his countrymen. His motto, *"amore et labore,"* has, in one sense, meant that he would share generously what he had of talents and material possessions with those around him, particularly the less fortunate. In keeping with this method, and motivated by the memory of his father and his concern for rural medicine, he traveled throughout Spain in 1965, interviewing rural physicians. His sensitive and comprehensive reports appeared in the *Tribuna Médica* and were published with the title *Por los caminos de la medicina rural* [Down the Roads of Rural Medicine, 1966]. (Later, in 1970, he repeated the sojourn, only to confirm that the situation of rural medicine was virtually unchanged.)

In 1965 he organized and directed the weekly literary supplement of *ABC,* the "Mirador Literario," from which he directed several campaigns. Through the Sociedad de Autores, of which he was once president, he was instrumental in establishing *casas de creación,* cottage retreats that would enable writers to work quietly away from the bustle of Madrid. He himself was able to purchase a small chalet (christened "Los Angeles," in the small seaside village of Águilas, where he and his family spend the summers).

Maturity and Fulfillment

In 1967 Lera received the Premio Planeta (the most highly endowed literary prize in Spain) for *Las últimas banderas* [The Last Flags]. It was a double victory for the author: not only did he receive the long-postponed recognition from the literary critics, but, as Frank Sedwick points out, "More momentous than its enormous acceptance, is the fact that this book got published at all, with the Republican, Communist, and Anarchist flags emblazoned on the dust jacket, and a bolder by far Civil War story than any other Spaniard and his publishing house had dared to issue in Spain."[8]

Such a success was difficult to equal, and it would be six years before Lera would be ready to publish another novel. Yet they were productive years. In 1969 he published the aforementioned *Los fanáticos* and came to the United States on a lecture tour of sixteen universities. It was also in that year that he began work on *Los que perdimos* [We Who Lost], one of the most difficult tasks of his career.[9] The following year, 1970, the Spanish Minister of Labor approved plans for the creation of a retirement fund for writers, and in 1971 Lera was named president of the Mutualidad de Editores.

His interest in other writers was extended to the younger journalists and students of Spanish literature. Appropriately, it was at this time that Antonio Heras, whom Lera had encouraged and been mentor to at *ABC*, wrote his artistic biography of the author. Likewise in 1972, when I myself visited with the author in Spain, he was very supportive of my research and was also assisting another student in her studies on anarchism. He told me, too, of a tour of psychiatric hospitals in Spain that he had just completed, and of his soon-to-be-published reports entitled *Mi viaje alrededor de la locura* [My Travels around Insanity, 1972].

He had also finished *Los que perdimos* by then, but knew that the timing was not appropriate for its release, due to the harsh realism of its contents. In the meantime he was working through in his mind a novel to be entitled *Se vende un hombre* [A Man Sells Himself], but had some fear as to his ability to produce another well-received novel. His fears, however, were unfounded, and the book, published in 1973, received a literary prize. With this new success, Lera proceeded to complete and publish his Civil War tetralogy within a four-year period: *Los que perdimos* (1974), *Noche sin riberas* [Night without Shores, 1976], and *Oscuro amenecer* [Dark Dawn, 1977]. These years coincided politically with the gradual transfer of power from General Franco to Prince Juan Carlos, the subsequent death of Franco, and the reinstatement of the monarchy. Lera's most recent book (1978) is the aforementioned biography of the anarchist leader, *Angel Pestaña,* and he continues to write.

Ramón Garcíasol points out:

There are writers whose life is more valuable than their work, others who exceed their natural vital currents through their creations, and lastly, those whose life is equal to their thought. I believe that Angel María de Lera is one of the latter: admirable in hopeful suffering, capable of beginning many times again; a man of healthy morality and a frank laugh; heroic bearer of trials that have tempered without destroying him. His life is an example of tenacity—after overcoming the vicissitudes of fate, both in war and peace time—a manly response to the challenge of life and adverse circumstances. After so much testing and martyrdom, he still laughs, and laughs with the clarity of a mountain stream, with a firmness that doesn't reveal, except to very sensitive ears, its melancholy source.[10]

In spite of the emotional and physical scars of the past, there is little of the bitterness found in younger writers. Not only does he possess the typically Spanish trait of stoicism, but he is still capable of affirming life. He says, "I love life passionately. I believe that the most beautiful thing is to open one's eyes in the morning and to say to oneself, 'I'm alive.' In spite of the pain or precisely because of the pain. Only when one knows how to suffer does one achieve the gift of the supreme pleasures."[11]

Those who have had the opportunity to meet Lera in his own environment attest to the same humanity, wide range of interests, and authenticity which one finds in his works. José Ramón Marra-López describes him thus: "An impetuous and impulsive man, always spontaneous, he leaps dizzily from one subject to another, with a haste and anxiousness to touch them all, with his characteristically vital impetus. And he likes to grab the bull by the horns, with the same direct frankness with which his novelistic characters confront their problems."[12] His home, speech, and his actions are congruent with the world-view expressed in his works. It is my belief that this unity of the author and his works, this manifestation of one who is true to himself, is one of the reasons for his literary success.

Chapter Two

Themes and Literary Creed

Classification

It is difficult to classify Lera—both because of his awkward position chronologically among contemporary novelists and because of his independence of any one "school." In this regard Marra-López observes that "two important notes stand out in Lera: his late and somewhat self-directed appearance on the margin of literary professionalisms, and, above all, his independence at all cost, without ties which link him with the diverse schools and groups existing in the country. Lera surged purely, solitarily, rooted in the most traditional literary Spanish Realism—adapted to the passing of time—and in which the Picaresque, Quevedo, Galdós, Baroja, and even Blasco Ibañez intermingled in their forming of an author intimately [Spanish], who marches alone among contemporary letters."[1]

Eugenio Nora[2] in discussing those writers born between 1905–1920, classifies Lera among the "pure narrators," those who are devoted to novelistic creation in accordance with the formulas of traditional Spanish Realism. Yet he concedes that the difference between them and those who tend toward the posing of intellectual or moral problems is slight, mentioning Lera in that connection as well as with those writers of the "new wave" (born after 1921).[3] Similarly, Antonio Iglesias Laguna[4] includes Lera among the first generation of postwar Spanish novelists (born between 1910–1920), the generation responsible for the resurgence of the novel in Spain. In attempting to characterize this group, he observes that its main contribution has been a search for what is authentically Spanish. There is, he says, a sincere concern for Spain and her problems, which stems from the Generation of 1898 tradition, though it lacks the latter's defeatism. Fitting to the case of Lera, it is a generation that is sometimes passionate, other times ironic; that pursues traditional Realism in most cases; that is influenced occasionally by

9

Italian Neorealism; that is almost always poetically intense; that knows Spain's historical and racial limitations; that is conditioned traumatically by the memory of the Civil War; that has little time for dehumanizing aestheticisms; that wants to come closer to Europe, and yet—as the result of prejudices, separating differences, and lack of information—does not become European as the generation following it does.

In his book *La novela social española,* Pablo Gil Casado focuses on the socially realistic novel that appears in the decade of the 1950s and is cultivated, for the most part, by writers of the "generation of mid-century" (a term borrowed from José María Castellet[5] and one that includes those born between 1922–1936). Yet Casado's book contains various references to Lera and his works.[6] Another label is that of Gonzalo Sobejano in his *Novela española de nuestro tiempo* (1970), who classifies Lera among the "conflicitives" (as opposed to the "social" writers), those characterized by an existential attitude or sensibility.

Some well-known critics such as Juan Luis Alborg (*Hora actual de la novela española*), Mariano Baquero Goyanes (*Proceso de la novela actual*), and Benito Varela Jacome (*Renovación de la novela en el siglo XX*) do not mention Lera in their works, in spite of the fact that he was an established writer at the time of publication. Alborg's work is highly selective; the others are of a more theoretical nature, and Lera has few theoretical innovations. Lera himself chooses to place his works alongside those writers such as Antonio Prieto, Andrés Bosch, Carlos Rojas, and Manuel San Martín, who, although born later (1926–1929), share his common concern—the search for a "new Spanish novel."[7] In summary, we see that Lera is included chronologically among those writers born between 1905–1920; that he shares certain characteristics with this group, but is also associated with the following generation; and that he has even been ignored by some critics. We have also noted that his novels have been classified according to their (1) narrative, (2) social, (3) existential, and (4) ideological content.

Narrative Art

All of the critical articles that I have read are in accord with respect to the narrative ability of the author. He is a gifted storyteller, capable of creating and sustaining plots of interest. Sometimes he develops as many as four principal and two or three subplots, each involving numerous characters, within the framework of a single novel. Luis Ponce de León says of him: "The characters of this novelist are true to life, in other words, vivacious. They are painted with firmness, with an impressive 'chiaroscuro,' with the most vigorous pen stroke, with a prodigiously strong individuality. . . . One must say that they are . . . formidable portraits of real types, alive, authentic, and differentiated."[8] Lera's wide experience and knowledge of human nature produce a full gamut of personalities, and his intuitive talent allows the reader to see himself in his characters. It is this communication with his readers which has contributed in large part to his popularity abroad, and as Ponce de León further remarks: "these characters have such vigor and independence that I would suggest to Lera that he put at the front of his books a type of name list as they do with the novels of Agatha Christie, or with those of Balzac. . . . He is creating a real human comedy."[9]

It is true that many of his main characters are similar to some degree (e.g., Luicano, Claudio, and Ramón, or Iluminada, Paulina, and Mercedes), almost prototypes of male and female. Accordingly, all of the central plots center around a love conflict, and although in some cases the result is melodramatic, it is not the cheap eroticism of the soap operas. Rather, in his emphasis on the emotion of love, the biological expression is sublimated in a mysticism that is more suggestive of the exaltation of creative intuition than of awe before animal instinct. And as Heras notes, "the physical love is a natural phenomenon. Lera doesn't linger in the sensual, in the superficial, because he knows that beneath the pleasure is unfolding a fascinating phenomenon: contrary forces, energies of opposite signs, that with their teluric collision are capable of creating another life. There is for this reason in this love the same sensation of fatalism that accompanies all phenomena of Nature."[10]

Thus he underscores the ritualistic aspect of the sexual union and its often tragic quality. For love is more dramatic when threatened by death or separation, as in most of Lera's novels, and as Rollo May observes: "Sex and death have in common the fact that they are the two biological aspects of the 'mysterium tremendum.' Mystery has its ultimate meaning in these two human experiences. Both are related to creation and destruction; and it is, therefore, scarcely surprising that in human experiences, they are interwoven in such complex ways. In both, we are taken over by an event—and if we try to escape, we destroy whatever value the experience can have."[11]

Yet this idealism, this rising above the "battle of the sexes" is a balance (if not a solution) to the underlying problem in all of Lera's narratives: that of unhealthy sexual repression.[12] Obviously involved in the twentieth century concern with human sexuality, as each of the main characters matures and achieves identity, they also acquire greater sexual freedom and integrity. Each novel deals with some aspect of sexual unfulfillment and lack of knowledge, and the antisocial means by which the individuals seek to escape frustration, namely: premarital sex, adultery, double standard, prostitution, and homosexuality.

All Lera's novels show an appreciation for the female psyche, particularly in her sexual relationship to man and her role to society. Like García Lorca, he astutely portrays women who are frustrated in their search for maturity or fulfillment, although these frustrations are found in the male characters as well. According to Brenda Frazier in her book entitled *La mujer en el teatro de Federico García Lorca* [The Woman in the Theater of Federico Garcia Lorca],[13] throughout Spanish literature there have existed three essential currents: the classical, the Oriental, and the Christian. As concerns women, her ideas are applicable to this discussion.

The classical woman is intelligent and astute, an individual in her own right. She is strong-willed, almost masculine, and knows her rights as well as her duties. Many male writers portray her in all their psychological depth, but mistrust her because of her astuteness and self-will. Lera, however, brings acceptance to her in the figure of Noemi and her relationship with Sixto in *Tierra para morir* [Land to Die In]. Later in Spanish literature the classical woman is idealized, so that in the age of chivalry she is an unattainable ideal who is to be worshipped from afar, taking on mystical qualities. Thus in Cervantes's *Don Quijote* she becomes Dulcinea, and we find her in Lera's novels in the figures of Minerva and Mercedes (*Los olvidados*), but humanized by the characteristics of intelligence and compassion respectively.

Continuing the classifications of Frazier, the Oriental woman is completely inferior to man. Indeed she is a nonbeing as well as a slave. Her survival depends on her hypocrisy, vanity, and astuteness, thus man's distrust of her. She is found in the Oriental tales of *Calila e Dimna* and evolves to the prostitute named Aldonza in *Don Quijote*. Lera's novels are filled with this character, but more often from the point of view of the "prostitute with heart," and often named María or Maribel, etc. Thus the Catholic duality of the cult to the Virgin Mary as well as the redeemed position of Mary Magdalene through love find expression in Lera, obliterating the lines of "saint and sinner."

The last category mentioned by Frazier, that of the Christian married woman, is also characterized by a lack of wholeness. For example, the wife of *El Cid* is a paragon of virtue, but she has no identity apart from her husband, spends most of her time alone, and is less important than her daughters. The object of the *Perfecta casada* described by Fray Luis de León is full of virtue, but lacking in intelligence, a quality yet to be recognized by society. Closely related to her are the two unmarried women in Don Quijote's life, his housekeeper and his niece. Both are upright, middle class, and lacking in true warmth and dimension. Lera too sees these limitations and seeks to remedy them in such figures as Paulina (*Hemos perdido el sol*) and Virtudes (*Tierra para morir*).

In accord with the existential position of the author, love is also portrayed as a means of escape from loneliness and despair and thus associated with the emotion of fear which Lera, in agreement with modern psychology, sees as one of the motivating factors behind human activity. All of the novels deal with one's reaction to this emotion and the results may be positive or negative according to the individual (e.g., Luis "el Fotogénico" versus Gonzálo in *Hemos perdido el sol*). Yet Lera sees fear not only as a necessary impetus to heroism (as in *Los clarines del miedo* and *Las últimas banderas*), but also as an incentive to bridge the gap between oneself and another. Further, the element of brotherhood or group consciousness is a constant in the novels, and each plot is set against the background of an actual social concern.

Social Themes

The *novela social* has been, up until the late 1960s, a dominant feature of Spanish fiction since the Civil War. Some critics, such as García Viño, would even say that a more exact term would be "social realism."[14] This latter term came into existence because the word "social" was often linked with the term "compromised," which implies an association with leftist politics. Because of overextension, however, the term social realism is still imprecise and lends itself to erroneous interpretations, as do "testimonial" and other words employed when speaking of this kind of literature. Therefore, for my purposes, I will turn to Lera himself, as his understanding of those terms will more effectively enable us to arrive at our understanding of his art. He says that "If the novel is the representation of man and his problems, the former being captured in a precise place and time, every novel must be by necessity 'social' without the author proposing such beforehand. My great preoccupation is the problems of my country. I was born here and I feel Spanish through and through, in good times as well as bad. Upon writing, I only try to help the people of my times."[15]

The social themes of which Lera treats are not only those of Spanish society, but of the modern world, contributing to the universal appeal of his novels. In many instances he was one of the first writers from Spain to introduce such themes and his novels have motivated subsequent actions to remedy the situations therein defined. *Los olvidados* was one of the first novels to call attention to the slum areas that grew up in large cities after the Civil War, although the condition was present to a degree in former generations and described by earlier novelists (i.e., Pérez Galdós in *Misericordia* and Pío Baroja in *La busca*). *Los clarines del miedo* [The Horns of Fear], although treating a standard topic in Spanish literature, is considered by some to be the best novel dealing with the Spanish bullfight[16] and is the only one to present the subject from the viewpoint of the victims of the system, a system which is gradually losing prestige and support in Spain.

Bochorno and *Trampa* both expose the emphasis on materialistic values in contemporary society. The former novel constitutes an early recognition of the discrepancy between education and the realities of society, and by extension, the problems of youths surrounded by adults who seem unable to live passionately or effectively in the world. This theme of youthful protest became a dominant world concern during the 1960s. The latter work (*Trampa*) was one of the first in Spain to treat frankly the problem of homosexuality, which is the subject of much current literature and universal polemic. *Hemos perdido el sol* was the first novel to confront directly the problems of the Spanish emigrants in Germany, and since the time of its publication, not only have there been measures taken by both governments to alleviate the practices of abuse and discrimination therein described, but it is also the topic of extensive journalism.[17] The other side of the coin, *Tierra para morir,* not only portrays the void left in Spanish society by the forced emigration, but is a forceful presentation of the repression by authoritarian institutions. If, in the broadest sense, however, the novels of Lera possess both social and testimonial aspects, the point of departure and center of all his works is Man. He says: "I never start from a particular situation in my novels, but rather with the characters. I follow their lives and they are the ones who give me the situation. I live them from within, not from without, and I interest myself in them as I am always interested in Man and his sufferings."[18]

Existential Themes

Important to an understanding of Lera's works is his philosophy that "the most dramatic and endearing quality in Man is his unequal fight with Destiny. I see Man as a crippled, weak, and contradictory being who fights, dreams and plans knowing only one thing certain: that he has to die; therefore the supreme epic quality of his existence. Naturally, every man, even the seemingly most common, is protagonist of this beautiful battle and carries within himself a dark world which the novelist must reveal. His behavior in the face of love, hunger, fear, death, anxiety, violence, affection, immortality, etc., is only a question of shadings, but fundamentally identical."[19] Thus, taking the existential situation of man as a point of departure has enabled Lera to transcend the limiting label of "social realist." Existentialism as a doctrine concentrates on the existence of the individual, who, being free and responsible, is held to be what he makes of himself by the self-development of his being through acts of the will. Therefore there is an emphasis on will versus apathy throughout the novelist's works. The essence of existentialism, Sartrian as well as other varieties, is its belief in the capacity of the individual to care greatly about this freedom and inner integrity, enough to die or suffer imprisonment if need be (exemplified by Gonzalo in *Hemos perdido el sol* and Federico Olivares in *Las ultimas banderas*).

Emerging awareness is developed through a series of crises which necessitate a choice. All Lera's novels involve a crisis situation and a series of dialectics or choices. Also throughout the novels are found leitmotifs such as a train, tolling bells, or other symbols representing the theme of time. According to Paul Tillich,[20] time is our hope as well as our despair and is the mirror in which we see eternity. It has the power to devour everything in its sphere and thus is associated with the theme of change. Separation from loved ones and from one's homeland are constants in the novels, the protagonists being "alienated" in one form or another. Yet change is necessary for growth and has many positive attributes. As Lera comments: "With the weight of the years and the lessons of life, one arrives at the conclusion that everything is changeable, fluid, shadowy. This does not mean to lose faith. On the contrary, it is to augment it, because it is to believe in more things, in more ideas, in more people, in a richer supply of possibilities, and finally, in the limitless perfection of the human condition."[21]

This progressive concept is also applicable to the search for one's self and for the absolute. The wisdom of all ages speaks about the road to our depth, and all who have been concerned—mystics and priests, poets and philosophers, simple and educated people—have witnessed to the same experience. Eternal joy is the goal, but it is to be reached by penetrating into the depths of ourselves. The protagonists of the novels are concerned with this search for self-knowledge, in spite of the agony which it often brings. The search in the depths is accompanied by a search on the physical level, for time also has the ability to drive toward an ultimate end and embodies the corresponding theme of destiny. In the novels of Lera, each person has a road in life and in order to be loyal to himself and fulfill his destiny, he must follow that road. The problem planted in a majority of the novels is that of an individual who intuitively knows his "road" in the face of social forces that want him to depart from it.

It is appropriate to mention here Lera's admiration for Albert Camus,[22] for both men are characterized by a strong sense of commitment to their inner truth. Lera, as is Camus, the author of *L'Homme révolté,* is a revolutionary figure or rebel—and these terms are used in the broadest sense to include any human being who revolts against suffering in the human condition. But both agree that the rebel must not seek to act in the name of any absolute values, but rather to put revolt, and revolution when necessary, at the service of humanity rather than at the service of systematic abstractions. This is the theoretical basis of Lera's abhorrence of the fanatic, expressed in the collection of articles entitled *Los fanáticos.*

Religious Themes

Lera decries not only the oppression of secular institutions, but also that of the church. Yet, like many Spaniards, he is not antireligious, merely anticlerical, and the Catholic culture is evident in his works. Furthermore, every novel contains images associated implicitly, although not explicitly, with the life of Christ. There is emphasis on the themes of guilt, sacrifice, and atonement, and an obvious protest against secular and religious institutions which victimize the innocent as they did the historical Jesus Christ. For Lera, as it was for Camus, Christianity in its essence (and this is its paradoxical greatness) is a doctrine of injustice, founded on the sacrifice of the innocent and the acceptance of this sacrifice. Yet, as Teilhard de Chardin has observed,[23] stoicism (related here to the Spanish philosophical attitude toward life and also applicable to Lera) is a belief in the validity of sacrifice. Thus in all the novels there are characters (major and minor) who willingly choose their sacrificial roles. And the "crucifixion," for example, of the matadors (*Los clarines del miedo*), the Republicans (*Los que perdimos*), and the Spanish emigrants (*Hemos perdido el sol*) is seen as necessary for the redemption of society (a restoration of equilibrium or at-one-ment).

Lera's attitude at this point is in harmony with that of Christian orthodoxy in its depiction of man's life as a "trial," and there are many images that reinforce the concept of "man in the arena." Yet he is not a Christian writer, but a confessed agnostic.[24] Thus his call to revolt is that of the humanist who seeks to transform the inhumanity of the world. Heras observes that Lera denies the dualistic view of nature which seeks to separate spirit and matter, and that "The conscience and the intelligence are for Lera, spiritual phenomena, the source of spiritual functions. As a consequence, no longer is there matter and spirit, but rather humanized cosmos and inhumanized cosmos. . . . Within man also there is a complementary dualism: the human and the inhuman, from which originate good and evil deeds respectively. The Universe then, from the moral point of view, is divided in three parts: the unhumanized (indifferent, amoral), the inhumanized (evil) and the humanized (good)."[25]

The response of Lera's principal characters to the "trial" of life is love, sacrifice, works, and humility,[26] in other words the ethical teachings of Christ, basic to all religions. Thus there is an obvious belief in the Incarnation or God Immanent. What then of belief in a transcendent

God of justice who rules the universe with love, and the God who is also a Spirit and whom we are to worship in spirit and in truth?[27] There is an apparent lack of faith in the doctrine of the Trinity (God manifest as Father, Son, and Holy Spirit). Yet there are a few characters in Lera's novels who are "true believers," as for example the old man Martín in *Las últimas banderas,* and José Manuel in *Los que perdimos.* Perhaps Lera is most identifiable with the character of the doctor Jesús (*Los olvidados*) in this regard. The latter is a more complex figure than the aforementioned Martín, and must struggle on toward the Absolute. There is faith in his struggle because, as Lera suggests: "Faith requires searching, psychic health, will, and humility."[28]

Literary Influences and Style

As mentioned previously, Lera continues the Spanish tradition of which he is an inheritor, integrating it with contemporary tendencies outside Spain. Of the former influences I will mention the picaresque novel, Miguel de Cervantes, Pérez Galdós, Pío Baroja, Miguel de Unamuno, García Lorca, and Antonio Machado. Lera himself confesses: "I believe that Galdós and Baroja have influenced me."[29] Those elements of the picaresque novel that found expression in the works of Baroja include the misadventures of social outcasts in an underworld setting and the themes of alienation, hunger, and poverty. The naturalistic tendencies are balanced by the Cervantine dualities of the "ideal" and the "real." And in this unique Spanish literary tradition, transmitted by Galdós, there is a tendency to view life from the point of view of the "romantic realist," to see spiritual values in even the most common forms of existence. Although Lera retains Galdós's epic view of history while recounting the inner histories of his individual characters, his novels are more dramatic in tone and are often concerned with the primitive passions. Like the painter Goya, he explores the darker side of man's nature, and like the poet-dramatist García Lorca, is concerned with tragic love, fear, and death.

With regard to existential philosophy, Lera's work bears comparison with Miguel de Unamuno's *El Sentimiento trágico de la vida* [The Tragic Sentiment of Life], and even some of his novelistic techniques, i.e., the emergences of consciousness portrayed in *Niebla,* [The Mist] and characters (i.e., Alejandro Gómez in *Nada menos que todo un hombre,* [Nothing

Less Than a Man]). Yet the Christian existentialism portrayed in Unamuno's *San Manuel Bueno, Mártir* [Saint Emmanuel the Good, Martyr] is more easily identifiable in the poet Antonio Machado, Lera's alleged model. Machado's picture hung in Lera's office at Aguilar (the publishing house where he worked as an editor) and his writings are kept on the novelist's bedside table. As Lera says of him, "never have such great things been said with such simple expression." The existential themes of the poet (time, change, death, destiny) are also present in Lera's works, as well as love for the Spanish land and people. And even though the image that emerges is often grim, painted with implacable realism, such severe criticism is made in the context of an enormous faith in the capacity of "España eterna" for resurrection and renewal. The poetry of Machado gives way to poetic prose in Lera, and verses of the former often serve as a preface to the novels.

The foreign influences in Lera's works are not as numerous, but include the Italian filmmakers Fellini and Antonioni; the Italian Neo-Realistic novelist Giovanni Verga;[30] and the North American novelists Steinbeck, Faulkner, and Hemingway. The influence of the filmmakers is evident in the cinematographic techniques employed sparingly but effectively by Lera, (such as montage, zoom, slow down, group scenes, flashback, and simultaneous narration), and confirmed by the fact that several of Lera's novels have been brought to the Spanish screen. In accord with the dramatic tone of the novels, an emphasis on dialogue reinforces the cinematographic effects, allowing the reader to participate in the events of the novelistic world. During the course of the works there emerges an ever-increasing mastery and progressively more frequent employment of this device (75 percent in *Las últimas banderas*).

The author is particularly successful at group dialogue that corresponds to a chorus as a background, and provides a complement to the solo voices. Words are chosen which emphasize the interior frustrations and repressed passions and are counterbalanced by others suggesting meaningful silences (all these techniques are used in the films of Ingmar Bergman, for example). Thus these dialogues have been categorized by some as being natural. Defending Lera, Heras suggests that "It is novelesque dialogue, not natural dialogue taken from a tape recorder, [but rather] with a literary construction which makes them more concise than the original. . . . In the novels of Lera, some of the dialogues may not be real, but yes, authentic. His rustic characters don't speak with their own defects and irregularities, as in regionalistic novels. . . . Nevertheless, the dialogues reflect the soul of these people."[31]

All of the foreign novelists mentioned as influences are social realists, if not protestors (like Steinbeck); regionalists who are sometimes concerned with a decadent rural society (as in the case of Faulkner); and whose works are characterized by a concern for the common man. Yet the most obvious influence, both with regard to theme and style, is Ernest Hemingway, the American writer who so loved and who is so often associated with the Spanish people.[32] Although he never met Hemingway in person, Lera's friend and colleague José Luis Castillo-Puche[33] affirms that the "old master" was much impressed by Lera's *Los clarines del miedo*.

There are many parallels that could be drawn between the two writers: the dual vocation of journalist and novelist; wide experience and travel; the close relationship between their lives and their literary creations; great vitality; etc. Technically speaking, Lera admittedly adapts the well-known formulas of Hemingway to his own individual art, and notes of himself: "I usually have no other preoccupation with technique than that of clarity, simplicity, and doing away with all that is unnecessary, no matter how pretty it may seem at first glance. I reject all that is not needed for the story, which I try to make direct, steadily progressing, and strive that, through it, the characters reveal themselves to us and tell us what they carry within. For that purpose, there is no better method than that of the dialogue, provided that it is always sincere, distinct and appropriate."[34]

Lera, however, is not a cerebral writer. For him the technique is much less important than the character. Referring to the creative process within himself he affirms: "When I sit down to write, one may say that the novel is already written."[35] Thus I agree with Heras when he observes that "Lera is not at all cerebral, he is only a novelist, a passionate novelist that fights to contain and administer an interior torrent of communication and creation. Behind his novels there is no thesis to be developed, there is an impulse. His narration is not an experimentation of forms nor a moderate and rational exposition, it is a paroxysm."[36] With justice Lera has been criticized, particularly in his early works, for a dangerous facility that leads to stylistic and technical carelessness, and for a strong tendency toward melodrama. But the mature novelist manifests an increased capacity for emotional restraint and mastery of the dialogue, and his best works exhibit an admirable balance and integration of form and content.

As with his personal style, the structures of Lera's novels also complement the thematic content. The closed outer structures correspond to the theme of crisis and stagnation, and to the ritualistic aspects of man's existence. Many of the novels are divided into twelve chapters, evoking images of the tolling of the bells at noon (related to a call to conscience), the hours of the day and months of the year (related to cyclical growth), or to the works of Hercules (related to emerging awareness and the epic battle). In like manner, the inner structures correspond to various themes and reflect a geometric progression of one, two, and three. The single element is evident in the central protagonist, the existential aloneness of each individual, and the point of crisis. Therefore all the novels have a central focal point of encounter, as, for example, Antonio's shock in *Los olvidados* or the den of Luis in *Bochorno*. The double structures are related to the man-woman relationship present in all the novels, as well as the dialectics or balance of opposites, such as the sun and shade of the bull-ring (*Los clarines del miedo*) or the contrasts between the German and Spanish cultures in *Hemos perdido el sol*. The number three in the progression is related to the collective environment, whether it be the village people of *La boda* or the inhabitants of metropolitan Madrid in *Trampa*. In a more restricted sense, it alludes to the circle of family and friends of the protagonist, or more simply, a chorus of figures voicing the traditional beliefs and customs of Spain. Although there is often conflict between these elements, augmenting the plot tension, all these elements are unified by a connecting-line motif symbolizing the continuity of time and events. This line or road is found, for example, in the procession path of the bullfighters in *Los clarines del miedo,* the subway in *Las últimas banderas,* and the Avenue of Menéndez Pelayo in *Bochorno*. Furthermore, there is a good transition between chapters, each leading naturally into the next, corresponding to the theme of emerging awareness. Finally, each novel ends on a note of hope and the beginning of a new cycle.

Chapter Three
The Years of Ire

The Spanish Civil War

The Spanish Civil War ended in 1939, but, like any other fratricidal struggle, it had consequences whose influence on the country can never be precisely estimated. Cessation of progress toward achieving a modern democracy, abandonment of necessary reforms in the social and economic structure, forced isolation from the rest of Europe for over fifteen years, and continued distrust by the European community even today are among the results of Spain's previous inability to reconcile the interests of its conflicting factions.

Indeed, the end of the actual fighting in no way ended the ideological conflict in which the Spanish were divided into two opposing camps of the right and the left—the victors and the vanquished. Spain observers saw how the careers of liberal teachers and professors were affected, how families were still divided on the political questions decades later, and how the children of those on the losing side suffered. The fact that amnesty was not granted until the mid-1960s is also indicative. The political consequences are history now, but the psychological aftermath of the war was perhaps the most devastating and the wounds are only now healing.

The war brought an abrupt end to the Spanish literary renaissance of the first third of the century and destroyed the atmosphere of free thought and investigation that flourished in the universities. Many leading figures of the Spanish intelligentsia suffered and died; many more emigrated to foreign lands. When novelists did begin to write again, led by Cela (*La familia de Pascual Duarte* [The Family of Pascual Duarte]) and Laforet (*Nada* [Nothing]), there was a need to purge the effects of war. Many novels reflect the desire on the part of the participants in the war—either as children (e.g., Ana María Matute) or as young adults (e.g., José Gironella)—to work through their own inner conflicts for the purpose of integration of self as well as society. This need is perhaps most prevalent today among the surviving Republicans who only now, after the death of Franco, are free to tell their whole story. Such an openness was seen in 1977 with the return of Dolores Ibarruri, "La Pasionaria," to Spain and is exemplified in the tetralogy of war novels written by Angel María de Lera.

Politics of Lera and the Tetralogy

During the last years of the Second Republic Lera was politically active, being numbered among the first followers of Angel Pestaña, leader of the Syndicalist party. Lera was secretary general of the organization and explains his position thus:

I am a socialist of the syndicalist variety. I believe that peace, harmony, and authentic social democracy can only be obtained by means of a syndicated democracy, to wit: by means of the agreement of men who create, because for me work is not an accident, but the rational employment of life. Only work—creativity in all its aspects—dignifies life and is capable of creating an ethic of decorum and dignity . . . Man is more important than society. As a consequence, the latter should be an instrument in service of the former, and not the contrary. . . . I believe that the efficiency of socialism should be looked for more in distribution than in the production of wealth, at least for now, until the mentality of man evolves and the capital sins cease from being the motors which motivate progress . . . each man ought to be free to choose his own goal; we should not hold back the most capable but rather make everyone begin at the same point—equality of opportunity—and help the weakest so that they can also fulfill themselves completely."[1]

At the outbreak of the war (July 19, 1936) Lera was in La Lina, near Gibraltar. Escaping to Málaga and then to Madrid, he joined his party and was assigned to the section on propaganda. Commissioned a lieutenant in the Republican Army, he was named Commissioner of War in Madrid, a charge he later renounced, returning as a captain to his battalion and fighting at the front line in Guadalajara until the end of the war. When the Republican government abandoned Madrid in 1939, leaving it defenseless, Lera gave pep talks on the streetcorners. He was on twenty-four-hour leave in Madrid when the city fell to the Nationalists, and he was arrested.

The cycle of four novels, collectively entitled *Los años de la ira* [The Years of Ire], is Lera's most ambitious work to date. In *Las últimas banderas* [The Last Flags, 1967], he reviews the war from the Republican point of view, particularly the last days of conflict in Madrid. In the second novel, *Los que perdimos* [We Who Lost, 1976], he documents the first year of his imprisonment in two Madrid jails. *La noche sin riberas* [Night without Shores, 1977] relates the worst years in the Prison of Ocaña, coinciding with World War II. And the final novel, *Oscuro amanecer* [Dark Dawn, 1978], describes his release nine years later and his reentry into the society of postwar Spain.

Las últimas banderas

Las últimas banderas, the first novel published in Spain to depict the Civil War from the Republican partisan point of view, won the Premio Planeta and was an overnight best-seller. Published under the censorship of Franco, the novel is similar to other romantic war novels, full of action with a central love story. Historically accurate, the main plot line incorporates the last days of the war in Madrid. The situation of the Republicans is untenable, for the Communists, headed by Negrín, have declared that they will resist to the last man, but Colonel Casado and Professor Besteiro are seeking a negotiated peace. The principal character is a young man named Federico Olivares, an autobiographical figure who is classified politically as a social syndicalist. Only twenty-two years old, he is Commissioner of War for the Republicans, who value him for his oratory ability. A prophet of sonorous voice and exalted passions, he is also a partisan of the enlightened dialogue—the revolutionist who would avoid violence. His love affair with Matilde, whose husband is lost in enemy territory, provides the romantic plot line. Olivares is related by ties of previous combat and friendship with three other men representing the diverse backgrounds of the Republican forces: Lt. Trujillo, a young officer with a wife and three children; Molina, the seasoned veteran and a high official in the Republican Committee; and, most importantly, Cubas, a peasant from Andalusia whose family was killed in the early phases of the war. Each of these men displays a different reaction to the present crisis situation. Trujillo, concerned for his family, seeks to escape, perhaps to America. Molina, the intellectual politician, will stay with his party, hoping for a negotiated peace. Cubas is related to Dolores Ibarruri "La Pasionaría"[2] and the oft-repeated phrase: "It is better to die standing than to live on your knees." Only Olivares, embodying the main theme—the necessity of choice—seeks to avoid making a decision and hides out in civilian clothes.

Structured in twelve chapters, the novel presents a binocular vision of the war. The odd-numbered chapters occur in the present and contain the central plot line, the even-numbered chapters revert to earlier phases of the war. Most dramatic are the optimistic days of the war in Madrid in 1936, juxtaposed ironically to the present in 1939, when the Republican cause is failing. Olivares says: "A syndicalist, a socialist, a communist or a republican think in very different ways. Our (republican) nation is a tragic, passionate element, and behind it there is nothing" (56).[3] At the outbreak of the war in La Línea, a village in the south of Spain, Olivares is with his young sweetheart Aurora. Her name is related to the dawning of the war, hope for the repressed people, and young love. She, however, like Matilde and many other women, is caught between two loyalties, for her brother is a Nationalist and her sweetheart is a Republican.

The principal focus is on the peasants and their united march against the garrisons, underscoring the author's admiration for the working class, which is evident in all his works. "They were farmers and fishermen, in shirt-sleeves or overalls, carrying over their shoulders pickaxe handles or pieces of oars. Invariably they marched in the direction of the garrison . . . they went tranquilly, some were even laughing and joking, but without rioting as if they were marching to work like any other day. It was precisely their gravity and unanimity which was most impressive in that critical moment of fear and general stupor." (53).

This unity and determination in the face of crisis are contrasted with the disagreement among their intellectual leaders, of whom the Republican workers are seen as victims, the sacrificed ones. And the atmosphere is one of a chaotic and nightmarish unreality motivated by passion and an overshadowing fear. As Olivares remarks: "It is he, fear, who is the cause of this upheaval. All of Spain is trembling with fear. It is fear who pushes us against one another" (63). A man named Old Martín, who helps Olivares to escape from his town to Gibraltar, is a memorable character in the novel. Martín manifests a profound inner calmness which effects everything around him, and he tells of his youth, travels to America and Canada, his numerous jobs and his many adventures. The lesson he has learned from life is that one cannot escape destiny, that the only freedom consists in choosing the path that is set before him. A man of courage and faith, he prays to God on Olivares's behalf and asks no payment except that his act of charity be repeated, if possible, by Olivares himself.

Madrid in October 1936 is described with images of a fiesta associated with the bullfight, war, and life itself. Olivares, having been named Commissioner of War, is summoned to Madrid. And his meeting with the Central Committee, including Largo Caballero (the Spanish Lenin) and Rosenberg (the ambassador from Russia), provides the background for an intellectual discussion of the war. The advanced age of the leaders, their condition as outsiders, and their ignorance of the realities of war are criticized by Olivares. Here too we are introduced to Molina, a bachelor and high official of the Central Committee. Ever the wise and experienced leader, he is a mature alter-ego to the often impetuous Olivares. His presence as one of the four principal male characters is a constant in the first three novels of the tetralogy, attesting to his perseverance and importance in Olivares's life. There are few personal anecdotes related to the character, but he is a major vehicle for the ideological discussions and predominant themes of the novels.

The Republicans are united in a heroic effort against seemingly impossible odds. Olivares, because of his oratorical talents, is instructed to unite the people, to stir them up, to provoke another "Second of May." This allusion to the war of independence against the French (portrayed in Goya's painting) corresponds to the mood of Madrid, a city raised to a feverish pitch of excitement and anticipation. The loudspeakers of the orators and rabble-rousers are like the trumpets of the bullfight, and the shouts of "they will not pass" are like great "olé's." But the waves of emotion produce a feeling of hysteria and unreality, and the theme of illusion versus reality is emphasized by the appearance overhead of a group of black clouds that produce the optical illusion of bombers in formation.

In yet another southern village of Spain, Cubas has already witnessed the outbreak of war. Arriving late from a meeting of the town Committee, he rejoins his two children and his wife, Clara, who is expecting another child—a child of the Revolution who will appropriately be named Espartaco or Esperanza ("Hope"). This peaceful scene, however, is interrupted by the appearance in the village of Pancho Villa and his followers. Representative of the opportunists of the Republican cause who pillage and murder behind the lines, he has come to carry off the three members of the town associated with the Nationalist forces: the doctor, the priest, and the chief of the Civil Guard. Cubas, the village mayor and a modern Sancho Panza, tells him that justice has been accomplished in his Barataria. Only one man had been killed, the former mayor, but the other Nationalist sympathizers now work for the common good of the people. The incorporation of the conquered individuals into the activities and structure of the town, reminiscent of the Romans and related to Olivares's later reading of *The History of Rome* by Mommsen, is a microcosmic resolution to the civil strife. The eventual failure of this hopeful and humane solution is foreshadowed in the following section, which occurs several months later.

Returning from the front, Cubas finds his friends and their families fleeing the town, which has been taken over by the enemy forces under the leadership of Paco "el Ditero." Notorious in the history of the Civil War for his Sherman tactics and terrorism, he had murdered Clara's brother—failing to accomplish his revenge on Cubas himself. The brother, as well as Clara and the baby, are portrayed as innocent victims of the war, for Paco had cut off Clara's hair as a sign of humiliation and forced her to drink a purgative which resulted in an abortion. Her own life had been saved, however, by the village doctor rescued by Cubas. Returning to the village at night with some of his followers, Cubas kills Paco and escapes. These themes of revenge and evasion, which run throughout the novel, are most artfully captured in a scene some months later that pictures the desperate flight of families from Málaga. The air of hunger and panic is accentuated by the pitiful cries of the children, and the frantic searching for loved ones is cenetered in the figure of Cubas, who later learns that his family has been killed by the bombings.

Lt. Trujillo, representing yet another aspect of the war from the Republican point of view, relives the famous battle of Guadalajara, in which he served under Olivares. The enemy were the well-dressed and well-nourished Italians, who were in ironic contrast to their bedraggled and hungry conquerors. The instinct for vengeance was strong and the Republicans placed one of the Italians against the wall, planning to martyr him. Trujillo remained insensible, paralyzed by his own fear, but the hysteria of mob rule was countered by the rational presence of Olivares, who restored order and justice in the manner of Cubas in the previous anecdote. All of these anecdotes of the past are impartial, portraying both virtues and defects of the Republican forces. Yet the voice of the author is clearly heard in the figures of Old Martin, Cubas, and Olivares, respectively, as they seek to mediate a peaceful solution to conflict. The fact that the magnanimity of these Republican men of honor was not repeated by their Nationalist counterparts is a note of bitter irony (perhaps prejudiced) injected by the author.

The romantic plot line begins with Olivares and Matilde in a hotel room. It is a few days after their first meeting, and the room, like Luciano's house in *The Wedding,* is a fortification against loneliness and outside danger. Seeking refuge in the past, the conversation revolves around Olivares's former position as a village schoolmaster. The children, symbols of innocence and hope for the future, must be educated to the realities of society, i.e., social injustice. They must be taught that each man has a right to the respect, aid, and compassion of his brothers, and a right to his individual happiness. These revolutionary ideas have not yet been accomplished, and each has the responsibility and obligation to humanize and beautify that which lies within his sphere of influence. The necessity for compromise in a cause superior to that of the individual leads to the dilemma of war. Ideally, revolutionary ideas should be accomplished without violence. for war signifies death, hate, and dehumanization, a prison in which Olivares finds himself fatalistically enmeshed. ("There is no exit as you see. This is the terrible thing: to have to use a method that one doesn't believe in. But I have not chosen it" [281].) He, although unwillingly, has a destiny, but Matilde refuses to commit herself to others, and is representative of those for whom the most important thing is personal survival ("The only important thing for me is to live" [280].)

The predominant themes of 1936—life, hope, and brotherhood— are united in a scene that is one of the most emotional of the novel: the arrival of the International Forces at the station of Atocha and the march down the Paseo del Prado. Representative of a united world revolution, they bring hope for one ultimate and cleansing purge: "One single battle, as terrible as you like, but one single battle, and it is finished. Like in a revolution" (283).

The dialectic of Revolution (idealism) versus War (reality) runs throughout the novel and emphasizes the lack of preparation which the author considers to be one of the major reasons for the failure of the Republican forces. The only element of hope in the face of the present disillusionment is represented by the possibility of evacuation to France or America and by the imminence of World War II. Yet these are illusory hopes, for the Spaniards are detained in French concentration camps at the border and there are no boats or money for the exodus to America. Even the outbreak of the World War is not predictable, and is related to the foreign powers' abuse of Spain as a guinea pig for their arms and military strategy.

The turmoil of impending defeat is compounded by turmoil within, as the Communists refuse to negotiate for a peace settlement. This crisis within a crisis is depicted novelistically as Olivares and Cubas are captured by a Communist patrol and taken to a makeshift prison. Yet the elements of compassion and brotherhood are present even here, as Olivares talks with one of the guards who had fought with him in previous battles (Teruel, Guadalajara, etc.). The older man gives Federico a cigarette, which he in turn shares with his fellow prisoners, and the incident is the motive for several anecdotes relating to the unifying potential of the tobacco. In many instances during front-line fighting, both sides had exchanged paper or tobacco, and even food and articles of clothing. For, as Cubas comments, "We are the same nation and it is natural that in many instances, many of us have shown compassion" (183). Again the theme of crisis is evoked as Olivares reiterates the truth of their existential situation ("we are alone, more alone than the number one" [192]). The necessity for sacrifice and atonement is emphasized by Cubas: "We need a victim and that victim will of necessity be ourselves" (193). The oft-repeated image of the crucifixion is embodied in the figure of Casanova, the Communist leader who, in keeping with his conscience, frees the prisoners and later commits suicide.

Released from the Communists, Cubas makes love to Maruja, a prostitute in a well-known bar on the Gran Vía. After the death of her father in the war, she had donned a military uniform and went to the Sierra to take his place, living with a young soldier who was also killed. Like Fina of *The Horns of Fear,* she is the whore with heart and courage, and is faithful to Cubas ("I will follow you wherever you go . . . I only want to be with you" [237]). Cubas defends her, voicing the philosophy of the author: "The only good people are those who truly love, with sacrifice. For me the only good person is one whose actions prove it" (238). Maruja is one of those for whom the war has ironically offered life and freedom from the enslavement of the village, and thus for her, as for Matilde, the end of conflict will signify the loss of love.

Similarly seeking consolation, Olivares meets with Matilde. But their sadness is related to the failure of the Revolution and their love, as Matilde confesses that she has long known of her husband's imprisonment in the prison of Burgos, and that for more than a year she has been a traitor working for the White Cross (a clandestine counterpart to the Red Cross). Again, as in the first scene of the novel, she takes a shower, as if to free herself from responsibility to Olivares and the past. And the latter, increasingly aware of his existential solitude, reiterates the theme of Revolution versus War: "I have been afraid to be alone. . . . I forget that I am a revolutionary. I never was a soldier, but I have always been a revolutionary . . ." (310). Although Olivares denies himself, following Matilde to her home where they are secretly making Nationalist flags, he is suddenly overwhelmed by the duplicity and immorality of his mistress: "She works for the enemy, with a husband in jail and a revolutionary lover" (316). The barely masked hate in the eyes of those around him corresponds to the Cain/Abel tension of Civil War and again evokes the image represented by the eagle in the opening verse by Machado: "The defeat that hung over the city like an atrocious eagle" (317). In defiance of this latter image, Olivares invokes the symbol of the flags of the title, which conveys the ultimate message of the novel: "The flags of hope wave on high forever, Mother. They are the last that remain for us. And who would be capable of definitively destroying them? No one! Do you understand? What does it matter then what happens to me?" (318).

Chapter 11 begins the denouement and continues the theme of feverish escape, as the Nationalist forces enter the city. In the streets appear a mixture of red and white flags, and a bustle of activity as families flee toward Alicante and the myth of the boats for America. Yet Olivares remains in his hotel room reading *The History of Rome* and does not succumb to the pathetic illusion of his compatriots: "This is the exodus. Flight again. Always fleeing. But to where? Until when?" (349). The image of a dead-end road is echoed in Molina's revelation of the terms of unconditional surrender demanded by the Nationalists. As the intellectual, Molina symbolically burns his books, among which are titles of Marx and Engels. It is a gesture which indicates the author's abhorrence of blind fanaticism associated with communism and all other "isms" that lead to inevitable destruction. The Revolution has failed, and many have died cruelly and needlessly in a prolonged war. Someone must pay the price; there must be a sacrifice.

The image of the sacrifice/crucifixion, extended throughout the remainder of the novel, is evoked by the presence in the street of the figures of a priest and a civil guard, representatives of the religious and secular institutions, responsible for the death of Christ and here aligned with the Nationalist cause. The theme of sacrifice is embodied in this chapter in the figure of Cubas, as he, followed by his loyal lover Maruja, is blown up by a mine.

Chapter 12 brings a rapid conclusion to the novel, as Olivares, like Cubas, must accept his sacrificial fate. The Nationalist forces have entered the city and in the streets there is talk of the men who are corralled like animals in the bullring, awaiting execution. The passing of a religious procession of penitents is ironically juxtaposed to a procession of prisoners, a symbol of complete defeat. Olivares, for the third and last time, denies himself by joining Matilde at the White Cross. But the feeling of solitude and despair resulting from the attempt to avoid his destiny causes him to face himself. ("It is useless to flee or pretend. . . . Now I know that it is not possible to choose. . . . Now there is only one thing left for us all to do: to save ourselves from the defeat . . . to give an example of dignity . . ." [403].)

The novel portrays both an historical and an existential crisis, the defeat of the Republicans. And the author is most successful in capturing the resulting atmosphere of fear and futile fleeing. There is an emphasis on the tragic quality of war, an historical drama in which the two antagonists are brothers. Yet the battle is one-sided, as with the Christians facing the lions. Accordingly, the Republicans are often associated with images of a sacrificial Christ, and the Nationalists represented by the Moors (p. 125, 238, 320, 337, 343) or alien powers (e.g., the Italians).

The element of sacrifice is also related to the revenge which follows defeat, and these two themes are connected with the several allusions to Goya's paintings *The Second of May* (revolution) and *The Third of May* (revenge). The theme of the civil war and foreign intervention is, of course, applicable to the recent experience in Vietnam. And the My Lai incident (like that of Guernica in the Spanish Civil War) will remain a blotch on United States history—a time when a nation saw that war traumatizes and disfigures not only individual men but, collectively, a nation.

Throughout the novel, revolution is counterpointed with war—the ideal versus the real, emotion versus reason—and the author criticizes the fanaticism of the former (the "they will not pass" of the Communists) and the cold dehumanization of the latter. The solution is a synthesis, progressive ideas implemented by practical means without violence. There is a need for true brotherhood and the incorporation of the minority elements into the macrocosm (as in the village of Cubas). The uniting element of humanism is represented by the mutual sharing of cigarettes, and the necessity for compassion is demonstrated by the action of the Republicans at Guadalajara.

The novel does not have the epic breadth of a Tolstoy, but portrays events from the point of view of a Republican soldier—an "inner history" in the manner of Galdós's *Episodios nacionales* [National Episodes]. Thus the true protagonists are the Spanish people, who, as Jean A. Schalekamp points out, inspired the admiration of the world. The sad truth is that the Spanish people have been the only ones in Europe who have raised up against a fascist sedition, that Spain has been the only country in which the civil population has confronted the military and has assaulted the garrisons. All the others in recent history, the Portuguese, the Germans, the Italians, and now the Greeks, have surrendered without moving a finger, so to speak. It is (historical) exception which makes the Spanish Civil War so fascinating and "romantic" for some.[4]

Los que perdimos

The first novel reads easily. The plot runs rapidly and the romantic element is a welcome counterpoint to the war motif. The last lines of the novel ("it was a long, dark hallway"), which refer to Olivares's entrance into prison, are also the opening lines of the second novel, *Los que perdimos* [We Who Lost]. This novel is of another tone, another pace, and another level of profundity. Written nine years later than the previous one, it not only reflects the author's own steps toward maturity, but his more demanding experiences during imprisonment. As documented in the novel, Lera entered a prison in the Glorieta de San Bernardo y Vallehermosa, in April 1939. He was interrogated and sentenced to death on May 1 of that year and transferred to the prison of San Anton. As is the first one, this novel is divided into twelve chapters, with a short chapter, 13, which serves as an epilogue, leaving the novel open-ended. Each chapter is introduced by a line from a poem which began with the previous novel and will continue to the next:

since in one single day / a thousand days are consumed or a thousand days were one / one single day of fire. I am the one to tell you, and that's enough / because I was one of the first to begin the task / and one of the last stubborn ones to abandon the trenches / with the other workers. At the end, we surrendered / without sun or moon in the sky / broken and without saliva / in our mouth, with our bones by the frost / by the hunger and by the iron and with our soul defeated / because of being neither alive nor dead and yes, nude and alone / in a vast cemetery where not even a grave did we find / to bury in silence the tiredness of a thousand days / and a thousand nights without our sleep. Thus was that work day / companion.[5]

The novel is unsparing in detail—the conditions are grim and the fight for survival is paramount. "A former seminary for boys in Madrid had been converted into a prison by the Republican authorities during the war. It was an old building, corroded by time and generations of students. The doors, windows, floors, and walls looked broken, dirty, and burned. It smelled like a sewer, and the gratings and bars gave it a sinister aspect" (95).

Crowded together, sleeping on the floor shoulder to shoulder, they subsisted on revolting gruel and food brought from the outside by their families. The daily routine included much standing outdoors at military attention, listening to Falangist propaganda or Mass. Unprotected from the heat or cold, many died and many more were executed. Yet within the limits of their situation, life continued. And slowly but surely they began to form groups of interest, based on class divisions, hometown alliances or political affinities. Hope is kept alive by news from families and possibilities of release. The overall atmosphere is symbolized by the necessity of raising the right hand in salute to Franco, with the accompanying "Long live Spain." These and other descriptions of the author leave no doubt as to the comparison with Nazi Germany, and indeed, in the next novel, with the Jews at Auschwitz. Lera keeps his balance, however, alternating between anguish and ironic humor, reveries of the past and dreams of the future. As before, he uses the technique of four male characters—alternately focusing on each. In addition to Federico Olivares (Lera himself) and Molina, there are Agustín and José Manuel, two new members of the group.

Olivares is again Lera—clear-headed and strangely optimistic, the romantic realist. The best scenes are those that describe (1) his confrontation with his accusers and (2) his relationship with his friends. In the former case he is amazingly cool in a crisis situation. His courage is equaled by his determination to tell the truth. In the second instance he is quick to share whatever food he has, uses his storytelling ability to lift others' spirits, and emerges as a natural leader among a diverse population. Nonetheless, he lets the readers see his human frailty—his fear, his doubt, his sexual frustration, and above all his painful agnosticism, which he displays with touches of irony. In military fashion, Olivares responds to the prison census taker. (Name: Federico Olivares Garcia; Age: 26; Profession: School Teacher; Religion: Agonistic; Baptized: Catholic; [89]). Initially intimidated by the sounds of those being beaten and tortured to secure incriminating evidence, he finds the courage to face the commanding officer, who in turn responds with nobility and justice, another of the ironies of war. Olivares's life is spared but he is given a sentence to life imprisonment, the low point, psychologically, of his experience.

Molina, the seasoned soldier, is another carryover from the first novel and Agustín is a newspaper journalist (a sometime profession of Lera's). But it is José Manuel who has the author's sympathy and overt affection and who is related to the theme of sacrifice. Only twenty-two years old, he is a Cuban, married, and the father of a young daughter. A poet by profession and a true Catholic in spirit, he wins their affection by his warm and gentle attitude, his poetry written freely and with great feeling for his friends, and his ability to make his faith believable to others. Toward the end of the novel Olivares is unexpectedly granted clemency and his sentence is commuted to "only" thirty years. But his joy is marred by the execution of José Manuel, with whom he so strongly identifies. The theme here is one of interdependence and empathy and is related to John Donne's reminder never to "send to know for whom the bell tolls; it tolls for thee."[6] José Manuel accepts his fate with equanimity, looking forward with certainty to an afterlife in God's presence, and is strongly reminiscent of the figure of César in Gironella's *Los cipreses creen en Dios* [The Cypresses Believe in God].

In a dream Olivares sees José Manuel crowned with red roses, wearing a necklace of rubies, and his white garment belted with gold. He is in a trance of serene joy, idealized. In his eyes intelligence shines, and his eyes are deep, fascinating, yet friendly and warm, compassionate, and tender. Speaking of his death and new life José Manuel relates: "I didn't suffer as much as I feared. One is tranquil when he realizes that the hour has come to free himself from what is called life, and which is only anguish, insecurity, and fear, a lot of fear, above all and more than anything—fear. . . . The firing squad acted with mechanical coldness and someone shouted: 'Long live the Republic! Long live liberty!' But at once we crossed the trench. On the other side it was not cold, and we found ourselves enveloped in warmth. Then I saw that my companions were recovering their normal aspects, many looked younger, and all were more pure, and luminous, and more, more fruitful" (388).

The embryo of the author's considerations on life and death begun in the first novel are more fully realized in this sequel. The spiritual and physical solitude is emphasized, along with the constant presence of death (here ironically named "La Pepa," to whom many jokes and songs are dedicated). In *The Last Flags* when the Spaniard was forced in the midst of violence and upheaval to take a stand and to assess what values

were most important to him. For many that meant loyalty to himself
and love. The man/woman relationship was the vehicle for love and that
relationship was exalted. In *We Who Lost* we find the same values, and a
deeper appreciation for the role of women in the war. The book is
dedicated to Lera's sisters and "all the women who console the prisoners
in the prisons of the world." He is also inspired by the women prisoners
themselves, those who share the fate of men. In particular, Lera
spotlights the figure of Dolores Ibarruri, "La Pasionaria," the most
nationally and universally known of all the women who participated in
the war.

As an exalted member and later leader of the Communist party in
Spain, she was the flag-bearer and symbol of revolution for more than
fifty years. Charismatic, dedicated, and physically impressive, her
exceptional oratorical ability allowed her to become the passionate and
convincing voice of the entire Republican cause. A domestic servant at
age fourteen, unhappily married to a coal miner, many times imprisoned, and the mother of six children, she is a remarkable woman who
lived out courageously a protest against enslavement of any kind.[7]
Although she began her career as an advocator of women's rights, she
quickly rose above sexual limitations to be simply a recognized and
gifted politician. Forty years old at the time of the Civil War, she was a
symbol and an idol who inflamed the people with slogans such as "It is
better to be the widow of a hero than the wife of a coward," and the
aforementioned phrase "They [the enemy] will not pass." Lera men-
tions her with respect and admiration in all the books of the tetralogy,
perhaps as a model of feminine dedication and courage, and perhaps
because he can identify with her life. In a rare personal letter in 1936,
she describes herself in these words:

"I have been a militant Communist since 1920, and before that, for two
years I was a member of the Socialist party. . . . My spirit was tempered in
the years of persecutions, fights, hunger, and imprisonment. Comrade of a
miner, I know the terrible pain of days without bread, of winters without
heat, of dying children without medicine. I speak for the thousand-fold pains
of the exploited multitudes, who are martyred and deprived of all happiness,
all joy, all rights. My voice shouts the rebellion of a nation that does not want
to be a slave and which carries within the depth of its soul anxieties,
longings, and desires for liberty, culture, well-being, and progress.

You have idealized me, you have ennobled me. I don't deserve so much. What merit or significance do my labors or struggle have compared with the formidable effort of a nation which is writing the pages of an epic, and which is sacrificing the best of its youth, the ablest of its men and women?"[8]

The men survive on meager rations and great ideas. Olivares affirms: "*Ideas son nuestra sangre y nuestro espiritu*" ("Ideas are our blood and our spirit"). The endless discussions revolve around the great questions. Why are we here? What is the purpose of it all? I have paraphrased the salient ideas of the novel in an imaginary dialogue between Molina and Olivares.

MOLINA: Do you believe that Christ did rightly—do the men deserve for someone to die for them?
OLIVARES: Yes. I have chosen love over hate. I have learned to love myself and to love my brother.
MOLINA: Are the ideals for which we fought worth the price that we are paying?
OLIVARES: Yes. The survival of the world depends on the survival of the humanitarian ideals of the Revolution—the early Christian martyrs are our example.
MOLINA: How can these ideas be implemented here in prison?
OLIVARES: To use what we have, no matter how little, answering at each moment and with each person the call for our best self.
MOLINA: Can we know the beginning and the end of human existence or even of our own unique life?
OLIVARES: I can't yet—but I have faith in an overall plan. Even when man cannot define God, he can follow a design for living based on love and sacrifice. Then perhaps he will find God.
MOLINA: Are you ready to die?
OLIVARES: No. I'm sure that I will live and that I have a mission to fulfill.

At the end of the novel Olivares, among a group of prisoners headed for another prison, joins his companions in a song to "*La Pepa*" ("Death") as the sound of the train wheels seems to intone the refrain "thirty years, thirty years, thirty years." The conclusion is persistently optimistic, in keeping with the predominant tone of the novel, and leads one to understand Albert Camus when he says that: "Some people do not clearly understand that what makes so many of us loyal to the

Spanish Republicans is not vain political affinities but the irresponsible feeling that they have with them the Spanish people, this people so like their land, with their ingrained nobility and their ardent love of life."[9]

La noche sin riberas

The firm ray of hope that ends the second novel is almost obscured in the third, *La noche sin riberas* [Night without Shores]. Similar to Elie Weisel's accounts of the Jewish holocaust, it describes Lera's experiences in the Prison of Ocana. Ruled by a diabolical commander, Chico Listo, whose terrorism is reminiscent of *El señor presidente* [Mr. President] by Miguel Angel Asturias, the prisoners fear for their sanity as well as their lives. Referring to this period in contemporary Spanish history as perhaps more bitter and painful than the years of the Inquisition, Lera states after writing the novel: "That was the way it was, although it pains us to say it. It would be useless to ignore it because it deals with facts and circumstances that no one will be able to subtract from our common heritage. It is better, then, that we all be aware of it; so that it may serve as a learning experience not to be repeated in the future."[10] The prologue contains the following verse by the contemporary poet Miguel Hernández, foretelling the survival of the protagonist ("Close the doors, throw the bolt, jail-keeper. Bind firmly that man: you will not tie his soul"). Yet the deep despair experienced by all is voiced poignantly by Olivares, reflecting the overwhelmingly fatalistic tone of the novel: "Was I alive? Was I dead? What has happened to me? God, what is this? Where am I, what have you done to me?' But God remained inaccessible and silent. I was definitively alone amidst the unknown, at the bottom of a night without shores, alone, alone, alone."

The opening scene depicts the prisoners standing at military attention while an obese priest performs Mass in Latin. This scene, also found in *We Who Lost*, is repeated at the midpoint of this novel as well as near the end, reinforcing its importance. As one of the major themes of the tetralogy, it is an anticlerical protest as well as a denouncement of the unity of church and state. Arising from the agonizing agnosticism of the author, and undoubtedly one of its causes, this profaning of religious freedom is forcefully portrayed. In a sequence verging on the bizarre and reminiscent of some of Goya's "Black Paintings" or etchings (e.g., *The Witches' Sabbath*), there is "a priest celebrating the supreme mystery of his religion in front of condemned prisoners who shout, protest and curse, and in front of guards that try to impose silence and submission to the rite with blows and slaps" (287). Olivares remarks: "What a profaning of the divine and the human! That, yes, was a black mass of a witches' sabbath" (287). And the sermon, a eulogy to Franco, invokes the image of an idolized Hitler. ("Fields, mountains, rivers, cities, and villages of this sacred Spanish nation belong to Franco, gifts that God has given to Franco . . . and everyone . . . ought to be grateful to the great man elected by God to save our country from the masonic and marxist criminals . . . enemies of God and followers of the Anti-Christ" [52].)

The prison setting of the previous novel is repeated here, but compounded, the severity of the situation comparable to that of Nazi extermination camps. Half a batallion (350 men) are crowded into one room. There are three toilets without doors or partitions, which do not always function, and one wash basin, which sometimes has running water. Again there is little or no food, except that provided by families, and the men are reduced to skeletons, literally starving. Ironically, the diabolical tactics of Chico Listo force them to struggle, as they march in formation, perform calisthenics in freezing weather, and are subjected to cold showers and lye soap. The only saving grace is a type of black humor expressed in gross profanities, a stoic philosophy, and a stubbornness on the part of some that enables them to survive. Hope is also kept alive by the outbreak of World War II and the possibility of Spanish involvement. Indeed, the war itself becomes a leitmotif in the novel, as the men play war games within the prison, planning strategies, predicting outcomes, and grasping avidly at bits of news smuggled into the prison. During the course of the novel Poland and Finland are lost to the Nazis, paralleling the gradual death of the prisoners. Yet balance is restored as England and France declare war on Germany.

The prisoners as well as their captors are described from various perspectives: the group as a whole, smaller groups of natural affinities, and individuals. Collectively the men appear as one gray mass of humanity, possessing both virtues and vices. The prisoners, as in any penal institution, are not above reproach; several betray their comrades for extra food or a cigarette. And the guards themselves are astutely analyzed by the author. Manolo, for example, is described as a "little man always ready to slap an inmate for any reason whatsoever, particularly if the victim is a tall, strong man and he has to stand on tip-toe to hit him. But he has one trait, rare in our circumstances, and that is honesty" (73).

Nevertheless, the theme of sacrifice and atonement on the part of the prisoners is a constant, as the author and they themselves attempt to give meaning to their sufferings. Describing a group of ten men huddled together in one cell, Olivares comments: "They were ten gray men, rather common, neither good nor bad, on whom fell the historic responsibility of a great national tragedy. Ten simple men . . . transfigured into heroes and martyrs against their desire, by a capricious and absurd design. Why did we have to pay for the errors accumulated by the preceding generation?" (19). United by their common vulnerability to death, they share an invisible thread of understanding: "All are expecting the same thing. All think unanimously alike. All suffer identical anxiety. The only difference consists in the fact that the look of those condemned to death is more constricted and anguished in some and more indifferent or proud in others. Nevertheless, there is established between all the prisoners, both men and women, a perfect communion and a reciprocated understanding that no language would be capable of expressing" (51).

Of interest to the reader is the division into groups and the inner political life of the prison. There is a sharp division between the Communists and the other Republican groups. Each has its leaders and structures aimed at keeping alive their causes and proselytizing the peasants who form yet another division. Grouped according to their respective villages, the latter are contrasted with their middle-class comrades, giving rise to somewhat idealized discussions of country versus city. ("In the country food is natural, loves and hates are real, the men have integrity like the trees and the rocks, and the women are humble, without trickery or softness, as it should be. On the other hand, in the city everything is a lie, a fraud, and imagined. . . . The men are half women, and the women half men" [54].) Nevertheless, because of their horror of bathing, their superstitions and colorful slang, the peasants provide what little humor there is in the novel. And the accounts of their sufferings during the war itself are some of the most dramatic (e.g., their being forced by their own townspeople to repeatedly run naked a gauntlet of chains and pitchforks). A last heterogeneous group is formed by the independents. Often professionals or of the upper class, they have strong egos, are unusually intelligent, and basically loners. To this general group belong Olivares and his friends.

As in earlier parts of the tetralogy, the author employs the technique of four men telling their stories. Molina, continuing his role as the intellectual, is a vehicle for discussion of the war and represents the equilibrium necessary for survival: "I write and write, and I think. Because of that I am, I exist. Unfortunately, I am and I exist, because it would have been better never to have been. Some day, perhaps they will understand their mistake and then will begin again. Fine. Let's leave it that way. Soon it will be two A.M. and I will call Agustin to relieve my watch. In the meantime, I will smoke a cigarette. And then, to sleep, in spite of everything" (191).

Agustin, the newspaper reporter, also reappearing from the previous novel, provides a note of ironic humor, a rational if not argumentative approach to everything, and is an avid food scavenger. He is contrasted with a third member of the group, a young man named Jesús. As a replacement for José Manuel from *We Who Lost,* he represents a similar position of innocence and vulnerability. Orphaned as a child and a cobbler by profession, he is married but wants no children, and is fatalistic with regard to his situation. All these characters are well developed, with dialogue and themes appropriate to their condition. Yet, as always, it is Olivares (Lera) whose life in prison captures our interest and provides the main plot line.

Because of his intelligence and photographic memory, Olivares plays a special role in prison life. Bits of newspapers are smuggled in with packages from relatives and he memorizes their contents. The war news is spread by an underground chain, and the group is particularly noted for reaching their comrades in solitary confinement. Like Cervantes, he and many others risk their lives for fellow prisoners and the bonds of friendship are often stronger than the fear of reprisal. Olivares, as a good storyteller, softens the bad news and embellishes the good, striving desperately to keep the spark of hope alive in himself and others. As a result of such activity, however, he is eventually apprehended and placed in solitary confinement for months. Often severely beaten, he fears to lose his sanity, but manages to survive by sleeping most of the time. A lighter note is provided by the presence, in the cell above him, of four women who whisper to him through the drain pipe. Whether the result of fact or fiction, or merely exotic daydreams, the sequence serves to underscore the healthy sexuality of the author and his psychological understanding of women.

The novel is softened to some degree by the feminine presence, both outside and within the prison walls. The most salient women characters are Alfonsina (Olivares's sister); Dolores Ibarruri, "La Pasionaría"; and Sister Gabriela (a Catholic nun). As representative of those loyal women who, at great sacrifice, bring food to those inside prison, Alfonsina sustains Olivares's hopes and is his main contact with the outside world. In reality, the conditions outside the prison are also grim for these women. As Republican sympathizers, they are ostracized by society, can find no work, and wait in endless bread lines for food. Under these circumstances many are driven to prostitution in order to survive, and consequently are rejected by their husbands and lovers in prison, for whom they have made the sacrifice. Alfonsina's story is more fully developed in the last novel of the tetralogy, but here she provides the motif of love and loyalty and will later be his point of contact upon release.

Another example of feminine bravery is provided by cameo shots of "La Pasionaría," whose vitality and charisma spread throughout the prison during her stay there. They had cut off her hair, broken her nose, and condemned her to death, yet she remained full of courage and politically active. The descriptive scene in which she appears is reinforced by the bravery of the other women prisoners, including some who have small babies with them. Also living within the walls, but as one of the prison authorities, is Sister Gabriela. Because her father's life was spared, she had made a vow to serve the Republican prisoners. So, together with two other nuns, and with the determination of a Florence Nightingale, she set about to bring some relief to the misery around her. The whiteness of her habit is contrasted with the darkness and grime around her, and in spite of overwhelming odds she is able to make some changes in conditions. The lice and fleas are brought under control, the kitchen is cleaned, and there is some improvement in the food and medical attention.

The positive feminine presence notwithstanding, Death is also a woman. And the death, by suicide, of Lopérez, one of the most colorful of the minor characters, is accentuated by his last bit of poetry. "I am under the infamy of the great prostitute / who enjoys the dark pleasure of excessive cruelty, / she who made Socrates drink the hemlock / who had Christ crucified, and who is called Justice. / But now the old wise fox is coming toward me, / death is she who calls me and caresses me, / she who disputes our fate with the enemy / and who, by taking us away, our liberty provides. / I already hear her steps in the silence of the night. / Hurry, don't delay, come near, our friend, / and let me lean on you" (194). Olivares, his spirit almost broken, also longs for death as, completely exhausted, he is transported in a crowded cattle car without air to yet another prison at this novel's end.

Not unlike Kafka's *The Trial* or Camus's *The Plague,* there is a certain degree of horror and nothingness in this work, as men and women seek helplessly for escape from their fate. Nonetheless, as in the novels of Elie Wiesel, there is a certain purposefulness to the suffering, if only that of a sacrificial victim, similar to those of the Jewish holocaust. The scapegoat theme is indeed present, as well as a certain dangerous passivity associated with the Jewish question. Nevertheless, this is a Catholic author, whose affirmation of the life and death of Christ is a constant in all his works. His anticlericalism notwithstanding, the figures of Jesús in this novel and José Manuel in the previous book, together with the resurrection dream concerning the latter, leave no doubt as to his spiritual roots. Furthermore, the novel possesses the particularly Spanish ingredients of black humor and stubborn tenacity as well as humanitarian values embodied in the major characters, redeeming what could have otherwise been an over-exploited modern theme. Unlike Solzhenitsyn's *Gulag,* this is more a novel than a documentary. And although it is definitely Naturalistic and sordid in detail and language, it rarely falls into the absurd. Stylistically, together with the previous novel, it is one of Lera's best. The dialogues, interior monologues, and observation of group scenes are artfully intertwined, providing a varied and integral picture from various perspectives. It is worthy of respect, both as a work of literature and as a testimony of the times, and deserves to be translated.

Oscuro amanecer

This last novel of the tetralogy, *Oscuro amanecer* [Dark Dawn], relates the sojourn of Federico Olivares, who, upon recovering his liberty and returning to Madrid, encounters a very different society than that which he had imagined. He had expected a hero's welcome, only to discover that no one has waited for him or accepts him or understands him. Time, which had stopped for him in prison, had continued its inexorable march for the rest of the nation. Consequently he finds himself out of place, forced in the midstream of his life to begin again. *Dark Dawn*[11] follows closely the biography of Lera's life as described in chapter one of this volume, and is also related to a later novel to be discussed, *Se vende un hombre* [A Man Sells Himself].[12]

The first chapter, a dream sequence in which Olivares has a personal interview with Franco, is one of the most artful and imaginative in all the author's novels. Employing a new sense of humor (corresponding to his release from prison), Olivares addresses the dictator in terms similar to those employed by the television character Mork as he speaks to his extraterrestrial superior. Instead, however, of addressing Franco as Your Fatness, Your Immenseness, etc., Olivares more prudently uses terms such as Great Chief, Grand Butler, The Master, The Great Just One, etc. Franco is portrayed as one victimized by his power, imprisoned by his office, and fearful of losing his position. Falsetto voice and small stature notwithstanding, he possesses the qualities for which he was noted, namely astuteness, attention to detail, and stubbornness. The topic of their discussion, Olivares's petition for freedom, is appropriate for all paternalistic attitudes seeking to prolong repression, and is an obvious criticism of Franco's prolonged reluctance in arranging for Spain's transition to a constitutional monarchy. The author manages a subtle irony, as the Father Figure tries to persuade Olivares how much more "secure" it is in prison, how he has plenty of time to enjoy his freedom later, and how he must have patience and wait . . . until who knows when.

The early part of the novel acquaints us with Olivares's progress since departing in a cattle car from the prison of Chio Listo in *Night without*

Shores. Arriving at Guadalajara, he is pleasantly surprised to find that the provisional jail is housed in a convent run by nuns and that his treatment is much less severe. During his stay there, which he ironically describes as being like a sanatorium, he learns of the fall of Mussolini and of the Allied landing in Normandy. These repeated news items related to the defeat of Hitler correspond to his own increasing freedom, as he is sent to one last prison in Zaragoza, from which he eventually receives complete liberty. Arriving in Madrid without money or clothes, he is taken in by his sister Alfonsina, who lives in a modest apartment with her husband and small child. The life of Alfonsina is not an easy one, marred by economic difficulties and an unhappy marriage, but she has survived the war and its aftermath and is a temporary support for her brother. Olivares searches endlessly for work, performing a series of odd jobs, mostly menial, and finds that most doors are closed to him either because he is a former prisoner or because he is too intelligent. The main interest of the novel lies in the colorful descriptions of Madrid, character sketches of multiple individuals, and unusual anecdotes of Olivares's (Lera's) experiences.

The romantic plot line is provided by his relationship with Celia, a prostitute who remains faithful to him. Her story, similar to many others in her situation, is told without embellishment. Previously employed as a servant, she worked exhausting hours for menial pay, and the death of her young husband left her an easy prey for the local pimp. She is portrayed as a complete human being with corresponding vices and virtues. And her sexual know-how enables her to restore sexual health to Olivares, who had been in prison for the last nine years. The love scenes are realistic, if not graphic, giving evidence of the relative freedom from censorship at the writing of this novel. Nevertheless, the romantic tone of the story is constant, as with Olivares's help Celia secures a good job in the home of an invalid. And Olivares himself is guided to health and wholeness by Celia.

Determined to keep his ideals alive, Olivares loses no time in making connection with the underground. He discovers that his old friends are no longer active, and that the younger members are immature and headstrong. Pursued by the civil guards, he finds himself once more in jail. Temporarily discouraged, he is tempted to remain in prison, but when released, determines to adapt and to accomplish his ends by peaceful means. Referring to his total nine years of prison life, he confesses that during that time he had time to subject his ideas to a long and severe process of revision, ridding them of what seemed to be an exuberant Romanticism. He concluded that against the terrible powers of the land one could not fight open warfare armed only with reasons, feelings, and humanitarian desires. One must take into account the relativism of each historical circumstance and the reality of the human condition. He further determined that "It was not enough to want something; power was necessary, and in order to obtain power, no other road existed than that of organization, discipline, and a priority of goals. One must say no to 'all or nothing' and yes to 'two steps forward and one backward'; no to 'simple desire' and yes to 'persevering action,' although one might have to cede on some occasion in order to be able to attack again, again, and again" (27).[13]

The conclusion of the novel and of the tetralogy finds Olivares working as an accountant in a small liquor distillery, after having turned down a teaching job because it was too closely identified with the politics of the state. Yet he is happy to work while he waits for a chance to voice his ideals, and is able to fight for his ideals in even this circumstance. Finding joy in simple tasks and warm friends, he states: "I would wait for the fulfilling of the great promises with my feet on the ground . . . and planting every day, not beautiful words which the wind carries away, but small truths, and insistently, like fine rain that soaks the land" (287).

On the Tetralogy as a Whole

The first novel (*The Last Flags*), romantic in tone and necessarily subjective to a certain degree, is nevertheless based on fact and balanced in perspective. Written fifteen years after the war, it manifests admirable restraint and is a fitting tribute to the author's desire to unite the "two Spains." As in his earlier novels, there is a unity of form and content, and in this case a greater variety of techniques (e.g., the four-pronged point of view and the alternation of periods of the war). Stylistically speaking, there is a greater amount of dialogue than in his previous novels and a more effective use of words that indicate silence, suspicion, or anguish.

The second novel (*We Who Lost*), written nine years after the previous one and unreleased for several more years because of political pressure, is definitely more mature. The language is provocative, the details unsparing, and the tone strident. Falling within the tradition of nineteenth-century Realism, there are astute psychological portraits of multiple individuals set against a detailed description of a socially realistic background not always pleasant to contemplate. More aptly, it is a twentieth-century novel related to numerous prison biographies, as for example those of Elie Wiesel, survivor of Nazi concentration camps (Auschwitz and Buchenwald) an internationally known author and lecturer. Having listened to one of his lectures,[14] I found him to be like Lera in the following regards: an intense preoccupation with his theme, yet moderate in approach; a compelling personality and speaker; a sense of humility combined with a sense of destiny or purpose; a profound capacity for suffering evident in demeanor and expression; and an apparent agnostic religious stand.

Stylistically speaking there is a leap forward in *We Who Lost* as Lera polishes the technique of four subjective masculine points of view tied together with the voice of objective observer. It is a cohesive work, retaining the interest of the reader and maintaining balance in spite of the subject matter. This balance is not lost in the third novel of the tetralogy (*Night without Shores*), but the tone is decidedly Naturalistic, with emphasis on the oppression of the environment and the inherent evil in all men. Verging on, but not succumbing to, the absurd, dreams and reality distorted by starvation and violence lend themselves to images and techniques employed by the Surrealists. Its writing and publication coincide with the death of Franco, and there is an obvious outpouring, if not regurgitation, of the most bitter experiences of recent Spanish history. The reader is forced to react and finds himself involved in the narrative, attesting to the story-telling ability of the author as well as the urgency of the theme.

Similar to Solzhenitsyn's *Gulag,* but not as long, it is more comparable to the television version of *Holocaust* written by playwright Gerald Green, author of *The Artists of Terezin* and *The Legion of Noble Christians.* Nevertheless, one might ask, why? We've heard it already; why again? In response to this question Gerald Green responds: "At the very least, I trust we will have placed a wreath on the graves of the six million, honored those who survived and paid tribute to that noble remnant who fought back. . . . [In *Holocaust*] Rudi Weiss survives by fighting, hiding, and refusing to go meekly to his death . . . that perhaps is the moral—if there need be one—of *Holocaust.*"[15] In a similar vein, the final novel of Lera's tetralogy (*Dark Dawn*) is the affirmation of a survivor, a survivor of the Spanish Holocaust. Combining all the earlier tendencies of Romanticism, Realism, Naturalism, and Surrealism, it is a fitting conclusion both in content and style. Furthermore, there is a new note of humor, albeit black or ironic humor. With the last lines of the novel—"I'm alive, I'm alive!"—the reader rejoices with the author in the victory of the human spirit over death and defeat.

Chapter Four
The Forgotten Ones
Social Background

Some of the most destitute inhabitants of Madrid live in outlying sections composed of shacks without water, electricity, and sanitary facilities. In the worst cases the dwellings consist of caves and lean-tos, often located in the immediate vicinity of sewer outlets and refuse dumps. Many of the people have fled from the poorer southern province of Andalusia, hoping to find work in the larger cities.[1] In 1948, on his daily journey to his job at the distillery, Lera witnessed the emergence of just such an encampment. With time the people of the colony came to confide in him, and Lera not only responded with a sympathetic ear but, because of his earlier legal training, became a type of counsel to the colony (writing their letters, filling out documents, etc.). *Los olvidados* [The Forgotten Ones] is the story of these forgotten people, an exposition of their situation within a society that is ignorant of their existence, and of their desperation and bitterness in the face of inescapable misery. Although greatly oppressed by their circumstances, they struggle to survive physically and even dare to dream at times. But their dreams are grounded in an implacable reality, and there is an air of fatalism pervading the novel.

Lera describes the inhabitants with fidelity, but avoids the sociological approach of the behaviorists. Each is seen as an individual, with a name, a nickname, and a particular characteristic or mannerism. They are not caricatures, but rather a clear example of narrative selectivity by means of which he succeeds in not only individualizing, but isolating his minor characters. For example: Ronquillo, "Money Wad," is "a fat and ruddy faced man, with a malicious glance and huge rings on his fingers";[2] "Don" Oscar is a mysterious man of unknown origin whose bald head appears over his tobacco stand, and from which position he silently observes the life of the colony; and Andrea, "the Countess," putting on airs of a grand lady, dreams of an apartment in the Calle de Goya, as she scrubs her poor adobe hut.

The stagnant cyclical movement of life within the colony is conveyed by the repetition of monotonous days in which the morning brings no light and the evenings complete the cycle of continual hunger and despair. Even the arrival of spring does not herald new hope, but rather mocks the seething living death of the inhabitants. The colony is not only infected with biological disease and decay, but also with spiritual misery, as in Camilo José Cela's *La colmena* [the Beehive], where the struggle to survive is characterized by man's inhumanity to man and only the fittest survive. This Darwinian struggle is further emphasized by the animalistic, grotesque descriptions of some of the women painted with brush strokes resembling those of Baroja: "Mallada was a masculine woman with a horrendous and hairy pock-marked face. She walked dragging a leg, broken at the waist. Because of her beady eyes, hidden among fleshy eyelids; her nose, completely Roman; her mouth, enormous and lopsided, and her wide and robust frame, Don Jesús believed he could see in her a carryover of the paleolithic female" (72).

Numerous descriptions such as the one above are reminiscent of Naturalistic novels and contribute to the air of primitiveness, emphasizing the alienation from civilization. It is a lawless colony, in the Picaresque tradition or, more recently, strangely similar to the leper colony in James Michener's *Hawaii,* although there are a minimum of rules for the welfare of the tribe. Yet even these people are capable of deep feeling and suffer under the weight of existence: Mellada: "I think, I think a lot." Antonio: "And what is it you think about?" (The face of Mellada becomes even more somber. And she who never cried, let two tears be seen plastered against her eyelashes.) Mellada: "Of what will become of these children with the father that they have. If I were a man . . . (Mellada also groaned under the weight of her destiny, and cried)" (73). There is also a cosmic interrelation between Nature and human life (Lera dedicates his most poetic prose to the Genesis phenomena of Nature). Thus if the animalistic is present in humans, the reverse is also true. Here the drive for survival is combined with the tenderness of motherhood in a sow, the only animal existing in the colony: "The most filthy, most clumsy, most repugnant animal was ennobled, suddenly as a reflection of humanity. . . . Then the blue of her pupils became more intense and bright and her tongue enveloped the small creature in a long and warm caress" (221).

Lera himself knew the joys as well as the sacrifices of parenthood, and also the agony of not being able to feed his own child. *The Forgotten Ones*, like Pérez Galdos's *Misericordia* [Mercy], is more than a portrayal of poverty and misery. For, like diamonds gleaming in a heap of rubbish, the lives of some individuals stand out against the background of squalor and point up the tension between ugliness/beauty and the real/ideal—the dialectics of Spanish literary tradition, which are a constant in Lera's works. Here the power of love to elevate even the most primitive to levels of sacrifice is seen in the example of "Cachopan": "Father love overcame his apathy and vagabond habits. . . . It was nothing less than heroic for him to work; but a heroism each morning, and then hour after hour, until the end of each day. 'It's for my son, so he may eat,' he used to say" (259).

While writing this novel, Lera would rise at seven, take the streetcar to the market of Legazpi, and walk to his job. Leaving there at six in the evening, he would then go to another accounting job in a nearby foul-smelling tripe factory, and then on to still another, in a more distant typewriter store. All this for a mere subsistence income, and a life in which even sleep is no consolation. It is Lera's own suffering that allows him to share so deeply in the tragedy of these people, and the novel is harsh, bitter and emotional—a literary shout. In this first novel his artistic sensibility will let explode all the pent-up thoughts, emotions, and experiences accumulated over his forty years.

Plot

Against the background of the collective protagonist, there emerge simultaneously the lives of the four principal characters, who converge at the colony from different backgrounds and experiences. Reminiscent of the structure of Pereda's *Sotileza*, the author employs a female figure, a beautiful young girl named Mercedes, as a focal point around which the principal male characters revolve. Antonio is an old anarchist, now voluntary schoolmaster to the colony, who protects her and with whom she lives platonically. Don Jesús, a friend of the latter, is a successful physician who offers his services free of charge to the colony. Mercedes assists him, yet it is her passionate relationship with Pepe, "the Granadino," leader of a band of thieves, that provides the principal line of action.

Arriving in Madrid, Pepe attempts various jobs, but the doors are closed (as they were for Lera) because he is too intelligent. This cerebral quality will be Pepe's nemesis as he is gradually isolated and imprisoned within the confines of his own mind. Like *The Double* by Dostoevsky, his dual personality is a product of urban pressures and of those inner pressures which recur in dreams. He ends up at the market of Legazpi, where he becomes a gang leader characterized by his audacity, cruelty, and obsessive desire to become rich. Yet there is a charismatic attraction that Pepe exerts over the other thieves and Mercedes. A rather stereotyped figure of unusual virtue and beauty, Mercedes is contrasted with the evil environment, and the author employs rather trite animal imagery ("dove" versus "hawk") and pathetic fallacy (the anthropomorphic wind becomes a "band of dark bats") to point up the theme of innocence and purity pursued by dark, violent, sexual forces. (These Lorquian techniques would be effective were it not for their overabundance.)

Previous to her arrival at the colony, Mercedes's life had been a descending spiral of hunger and misery as she witnessed the gradual death of her mother—a victim of overwork, cancer, and an animalistic second husband. Molested by her stepfather, she flees to the colony, where she is taken in by Antonio. In contrast to the more primitive women who are able to adapt to the environment (e.g., Crucita) and in some cases who are even stronger than their male counterparts (e.g., Mellada). Mercedes is exemplary of the nineteenth-century woman who is threatened by the environment and whose only hope is marriage. There is a Madonna-like quality about her that is also found in the other women characters whose name begin with "M" (Minerva, Magdalena, and Martina); and the archetypal significance of the Virgin Mary as the perfected example of womanhood is seen in each of them, with the particular distinction which their name implies. Envied by the other women and fearing the lust of the men, Mercedes is an isolated figure whose soul instinctively withdraws from the hostile environment. Her aloofness stems from a determination to maintain her dignity and even to nourish dreams of beauty. Thus, temporarily protected by Antonio, she waits for an open door to freedom and a new way of life.

Pepe's pursuit of Mercedes is, fittingly, a study in "machismo."[3] The swaggering fearlessness and brutal control which he holds over the gang of thieves is paralleled in his disdainful domination of Mercedes, yet is only the outer manifestation of an underlying sense of inadequacy and fear. The plot traces their passionate love affair from its inception to its demise, but in a deeper sense, it portrays the ultimate consequences of a frustrated escape from a solitary fate. The marriage is endlessly postponed pending the last desperate attempt of Pepe to become rich by robbery. The anticlimax is the assault on the robbery victim, which results in Pepe's arrest. Mercedes, who is pregnant, sees the child as a ray of hope, but this momentary illusion is soon shattered when she goes to the jail, only to witness the complete splitting of Pepe's personality—an isolation from society and from an understanding of himself, Pepe's cell is an enclosure synonymous with his own mind, from which he was never able to escape, and Mercedes dies in premature childbirth despite the tender care of the doctor.

As is evident from the above résumé, the plot is dangerously close to melodrama, and indeed, some of the scenes are definitely overstated (e.g., the death scene). But there are autobiographical elements in the story of Mercedes that make the emotionalism understandable if not commendable. Lera's own mother and three sisters suffered many hardships because of the early death of his father, the struggle for existence during the war years, and the ostracism resulting from Lera's imprisonment. His mother died a slow death from Parkinson's disease, and his favorite younger sister died in childbirth.

Antonio

Although the plot has sustaining interest and provides a unifying thread, a large part of the novel (by means of flashback) acquaints the reader with the past lives of the main characters. Of particular interest to the reader is the story of Antonio. The character is a synthesis of two persons from real life: Antonio Pareja (a prison companion of the author's) and Lera himself.[4] The novelist spent a good portion of his childhood in the home of his paternal grandfather, an austere gentleman of scrupulous morals who imposed strict discipline and rigid religious observances, which included a study of the lives of the saints and apostles. At the age of eleven Lera entered the Seminary of Vitoria, where the reading and meditation of the Gospels saturated him with mysticism. But the exalted spiritualism was interrupted by the death of his father, which left his mother and three sisters with only a small pension. His decision to leave the seminary at age seventeen was the result of a religious crisis; one without interior violence, but which, inexplicably, left him with a complete insensibility to that which had previously obsessed him. Giving private lessons to help support his family, he came face to face with women and social injustice. His religious ardor was now a man-oriented one, as he devoted himself passionately to the cause of social equality.

The life of the novelistic character, Antonio, is closely related to the above biographical interpolation. Raised in an orphanage in Sevilla, he later entered an austere, contemplative monastery. Inspired by his love for God and humanity, he went out to preach the Gospel to the masses, but they drove him from the villages "like a crazy man or an idiot." Quixotic images are associated with this figure throughout the narration, and echoed in his physical description at the time of his arrival at the colony. "He was an extraordinarily thin man, but without any appearance of decrepitude. One would judge him to be in the beginnings of the winter of his life; but when he looked at you and smiled, so much light flowed from his eyes, that he gave the sensation of being a young man prematurely aged" (21).

Antonio soon came to the conclusion that *agape* ("love") alone was not the solution. Thus, with social justice as his goal, he (like the real-life Antonio Pareja) became an anarchist; and the personal sacrifices and political activities which followed are essentially those which occurred to Pareja.[5] His charisma brought him the adoration of the women, of whom he was seemingly oblivious. His only acquaintance with romantic love was both tragic and prophetic, the turning point of his life. Appropriately named Minerva, the girl was the daughter of an intellectual anarchist, but she represented a threat to his ideal of dedication and self-sacrifice. Destiny would have them meet briefly in Madrid, where both were teachers and both were alone. Antonio's subsequent arrest and macabre punishment—to be led during the course of a year from jail to jail across la Mancha—intensifies both the Quixotic and circular images of the narrative; but is also symbolic of Lera's own prison experiences. Upon arriving in Madrid, the idealistic man of action had died, and the contemplative fatalist had been born. His teaching activities there were interrupted by the war, and after a series of numerous and diverse jobs, the eternal wanderer, like Lera, came to rest at the end of the world, the lawless colony.

His life in the colony, when the story begins, is reminiscent of another Antonio—Antonio Machado. He is a silent and solitary figure whose simple, unadorned existence will later be mirrored in his lonely death. His evenings are spent correcting the papers of his nonpaying students and writing in his diary. His door is always open, and his daily bread, more often than not, used for the nourishment of others. In his walks through the colony he often seeks the solace of the river, and he is haunted by dreams and memories of a lost love and the melancholy of a forgotten youth. Seeking peace in the abolishment of all desire, he is again able to deny love, when in a moment of desperation Mercedes begs him to marry her. But this moment is the beginning of a rapid descent, as Antonio deteriorates physically and mentally. Suffering from hallucinations and insomnia, he experiences an indefinable longing. His death occurs by the river, under a star-filled sky, and a purifying blanket of snow.

Don Jesús

The character of don Jesús is inspired by a real person, a physician who dedicated his mornings to attending the people of the colony, and also recalls aspects of Lera's father and other rural doctors whose lives are described in *Por los caminos de la medicina rural* [Down the Roads of Rural Medicine]. "A hero is inconceivable without fear, because it is fear that creates him, and if the doctor were a perfect being he would not be *human,* which is his highest quality. Because of his humanity the doctor is characterized, beyond his scientific ability, by an irresistible *vocation* and an extraordinary capacity for *love* and *sacrifice.* Even greater than the *poets* is his overflowing heart"[6] (italics mine). The qualities above are all found in don Jesús. Like Galdos's figure of Benina in *Misericordia*, he is a person of great energy whose sacrifices stem from pure motives and who lives passionately in the present: "It was a work of wild intensity, but he performed it with real enthusiasm, not as a sacrifice, but with the pleasure of one who releases a tremendous pressure of the spirit" (123). The image of a conqueror fighting an epic battle against the enemy is reinforced by several allusions to Einstein, and his Jewish origin further links him to the biblical prophet-poets.

There is much of the mature Lera in this character, and his conversations with Antonio echo the philosophical preoccupations of the author at that time (a dialogue between Lera and Himself). The novelistic character does not develop during the course of the narrative, and there are no flashbacks to his past life. But he is the only major character who survives, and his constancy and balanced life permit him to represent the final message of the novel. His importance is further underlined by the pattern of his appearance in the work: his conversations with Antonio occur in the middle of both Part I and Part II, and he is alone in the closing scene of Part I and at the close of the novel, Part III.

Antonio and don Jesús are linked together by a common bond of intelligence and sensibility and their love for Mercedes, but also by a shared sense of melancholy and frustration (an expression of Lera's own sense of unfulfillment at the time). "Their spirits navigated in unison through a nebulous sea of melancholy. The two felt equally frustrated, and although in the physician there was still a lively curiosity for everything, in contrast with the passive indifference of the old anarchist, in both of them there gravitated the *tiredness* of the days. They saw themselves as old, *incinerated by time*. [They were] like two witnesses of the sad human comedy, silent and inoperative" (114), (italics mine).

This melancholy of maturity is expressed in Georg Lúkacs's theory of the contemporary novel, which, to him, seems to inherit the tradition of the classic tragedy, demonstrating the insignificance of our powers in the face of the task that we see ourselves impelled to attempt and the forces that oppose us (cf. Lera's "unequal fight with Destiny" cited in Chapter 2). According to Lúkacs, the novel is the fruit of a mature virility and is characterized by irony and melancholy, as seen in Cervantes and his mature work, *Don Quijote*.[7] In his awareness of life's ironies, don Jesús is almost cynical, while Antonio seems a personification of Albrecht Dürer's etching entitled *Melancholy*.

Meaning

The Forgotten Ones is a small human comedy, reflecting the condition of man and his reaction to his circumstances. The portrayal of the lawless colony as being "at the end of the world" has a leveling effect which equalizes all the inhabitants in an existential limit situation. Confronted with the misery of their situation, the individuals of the colony will either sink into passivity or affirm their wills. This dialectic of apathy versus action is represented by Antonio ("Let's don't try to cross over the mountain peaks. It is better to follow the line of the valleys" [111]) and don Jesús ("One must desire something ardently" [110]. But the note of fatality is strengthened by the ironic failures of those in the colony who attempt to impose their wills positively: Romauldo, inspired by love for his son, overcomes his apathy, only to be killed in an accident; Emilio struggles to become an accountant, with little or no possibility for success; Magdalena perfects her sewing skills, but becomes blind; Mercedes loved Pepe, but dies in childbirth; and Antonio's self-sacrifice only leads to a lonely death. This air of fatalism pervades the novel and is a reflection of the author's philosophical point of view at the time of writing: "Men are divided into two types or castes, according to the sign under which they are born; positive men and negative men; superior men or lesser men. This sign determines a whole life, a whole destiny, without will being able to prevail against it" (24).

The novel is also concerned with man's frustrated attempts to escape his loneliness by means of the love union. The affair of Pepe and Mercedes has a tragic end, as do most of the passionate love relationships in Lera's works, and the unity of love and death is emphasized. Antonio and Mercedes denied themselves of happiness because of high ideals, and don Jesús's wife, Sara, is an example of living death, as she has lost her memory. The final vision of the wintry death of Antonio is a seemingly pessimistic one, and the Lúkacs mixture of irony and melancholy is found in the last lines of the novel: "Two tears had remained frozen on his eyelids. And the men of justice believed that that man was crazy" (303). But there is a ray of hope in the permanence of don Jesús, whose eyes are looking ahead. Thus the ending may be regarded as a yielding to poetic uncertainty rather than a surrender to the ideal of nothingness, and is an expression of the agnostic position of Lera.

Criticism

The Forgotten Ones was recognized by the critics only with its second edition (1961) and after the success of his second novel, *Los clarines del miedo* [The Horns of Fear, 1958]. The critic José Ramón Marra-López is typical of those who see both virtues and defects in the novel.[8] Although he hastens to assert that there is "an account of truth difficult to forget" in the work, he also notes a "series of naivetés which, although expected in a first work, prevent it from jelling into a great novel in spite of the human importance of the theme." He further notes a "lack of rigor in the language which makes it fall into a series of set phrases that detract from the text."

The author employs the third-person point of view interspersed with dialogue, but the dialogued sequences are relatively few in number, and the author is too much present (although his is a restricted omniscience). The flashbacks (printed in italics) use the same invariable combination, which is not always appropriate, as each is motivated by a different situation. For example, Antonio is alone, the solitary reflection being touched off by Mercedes's appearance in his life; but Mercedes is in the presence of Antonio, a confession situation similar to that of Pepe in the presence of Mercedes. These flashbacks, although interesting for the most part, are too long and detract from the tension of the novel, resulting in a separation of the characters from the background. Another disunifying element is the digression concerning the arrival of the gypsies and the tourists. Although included for the purpose of contrast (with the preceding climactic tension of the plot line, and also with the colony, emphasizing its isolation), it is a jarring note that does not mesh with the whole. There is also a peculiarly cinematographic effect, which will be used more effectively in later works. But here the camera swings wildly through time and space, redeemed only by some excellent "close-ups" (e.g., Crucita in the refuse dump and Antonio's kiss on Mercedes's throat) and some group scenes (e.g., don Jesús's walk through the colony). Stylistically speaking, there are an overabundance of grotesque, decaying images (e.g., sewer, pus, worm), and in general an overall wordiness. The author shows a tendency to abuse the tripartite construction in adjectives and phrases, but has an extensive vocabulary and a tremendously forceful pen, which, when tamed, results in a vital flowing prose. The poetic element is present here also, and there are lovely lyrical passages devoted to nature.

As noted, *The Forgotten Ones* is written in a manner derived from Spanish literary tradition, from the picaresque novel to García Lorca. It is a sociopsychological novel with traces of Galdós, Baroja, and Unamuno, and contains the philosophical ideas of the late nineteenth and early twentieth century. In some ways it is similar to the Generation of 1898's examination of conscience (a characteristic of the contemporary social novel), and is also comparable to the spiritual Naturalism of Galdós. But although Lera shares the latter's compassion for his characters, he lacks his humor. There is a directness, a harshness, and an accusatory testimonial that are the result of direct involvement with, and not only observation of, the people and circumstances described. This emotional involvement leads to melodrama in some instances, and causes major characters to be strangely separated from the background environment. Attempting to combat the sordid environment of the colony, he allows his protagonists to become idealized, despite the interest they hold for the reader. Yet Lera transmits his passion and vitality, and the honesty and authenticity of the work are indisputable. For a first novel, it is surprisingly good. Many elements of his later novelistic work are to be found here and *Los olvidados* is of particular interest because of the autobiographical elements and philosophy of the author therein contained.

Chapter Five

The Horns of Fear
and The Wedding

The two novels—*Los clarines del miedo* [The Horns of Fear] and *La Boda* [The Wedding]—under consideration in this chapter are complementary in three ways: both have a rural setting, a tragic plot, and revolve around a blood ritual. The two villages, in the regions of la Mancha and la Rioja, respectively, are related to Lera's childhood and a search for cultural and psychological roots. And, as Marra-López points out (referring to *The Wedding*), they also contain the roots of Spain itself. He says: "This village is representative of any village of Spain, hard and mountainous, and a preserver of a thousand customs and a barbaric mentality."[1] The theme of barbarism versus civilization is prominent in both novels, particularly in the mixture of pagan and religious customs and in the reiteration of the "black Spain" theory.[2] The hermeticism and superstition that hinder growth and fulfillment are seen in the representative characters of the villages, by means of whom Lera offers indirect social criticism.

Both novels are tragedies, the protagonists betrayed by flaws in their own characters and also by the villagers, who consider them to be outsiders. Appropriately, both protagonists have a nickname that means "the black one," although in reality they are Caucasians. The structures are suitable to the tragedy, as they are intense, dramatic, and tightly constructed. Both observe the dramatic unities of time and space and are divided into sections corresponding to the structure of the day (twelve hours in *Clarines*; morning, afternoon, and evening in *Boda*). As in Greek tragedies, there is a form of chorus (a role played by the villagers), and in some instances, the violence occurs offstage. Both are peculiarly Spanish, involving the honor theme of the Golden Age drama of Lope and Calderón, and in some ways similar to García Lorca's rural tragedies, particularly *Bodas de sangre* [Blood Wedding]. Finally, they possess a universality and humanism related to Shakespeare's works, in this instance, *Othello.*

The two rituals around which the works revolve are a bullfight and a wedding, respectively, with emphasis on the purifying effect of blood-spilling. Although the bullfight represents man's confrontation with death, and the marriage, his encounter with love, they both have sacrificial/sacramental elements and are related to man's deepest needs and fears.[3] As in the function of the tragedy itself, the rituals have a purging effect on the participants as well as the spectators, allowing a release of pent-up violence and sexuality. A strong note of irony, particularly in *The Horns of Fear,* is reinforced by the predominant ironic tone and by the surprise endings.

Both novels have several subplots and present an involved development of major characters.

Los clarines del miedo

Although there has been a vast amount of literature dealing with the bullfight, most of it has glorified the phenomenon, as for example in García Lorca's poem *Llanto por la muerte de Ignacio Sánchez Mejías* [Lament for the Death of Ignacio Sánchez Mejías] and Blasco Ibáñez's novel *Sangre y arena* [Blood and Sand].[4] Some of the best works on the subject have been written by foreigners (e.g., Ernest Hemingway's *Death in the Afternoon*), perhaps because of a certain objectivity Lera himself has been able to achieve for the reason that he is not an ardent fan. Written from memories of his youth in the provinces, the novel is largely the result of intuition (which, according to Lera, is 70 percent of literary creation).[5] The inspiration for the theme came from a reproduction of Zuloaga's *Toreros de pueblo,* and suggests a beautiful etching in the tradition of the Spanish painters Goya, Zuloaga, and Solana.

Not only is there an objective distance between the subject and the author, but the point of view is completely antitopical. As is his custom, the novelist boldly confronts the situation, probing to its source. Thus the essence of the *fiesta negra* is to be found in its origins; not in the glory of the *corridas* of the large cities, but in the small Spanish towns and the barbaric, primitive *capeas.* Here the bull-ring is an improvised arrangement of carts and planks in the Plaza Mayor, and the bulls, more dangerous because of their age and experience, are in contrast to the young and inexperienced matadors. Driven by desperate hunger and dreams of money and fame, their situation is a tragically ironic one because: "in the profession of matador one begins at the end, doing, as an apprentice, what no one would dare to do as a master."[6] The paradoxes of the institution are a reflection of life itself, and one of the main themes of the novel.

Like *The Forgotten Ones,* this is the personal history of "the heroes of hunger and fear" (to whom the book is dedicated), those whom "no one remembers because they did not achieve fame. Many of them, nevertheless, left their life in the bull-ring, and all of them, their youths." The background setting, an indeterminate village of Cervantes's la Mancha, is a living, integral part of the work, both harmonizing with and explaining the ritual of the bullfight. The austerity of the landscape, the stifling heat, and the burning sun—all are representative of a primitive mode of existence, where barbaric cruelty and stoic humanism exist side by side, whose repressed aggressions and sexuality are released only once a year in an explosion of passions, which is the Fiesta. The Fiesta is the reason for being and the point of departure of the novel, which takes place between the early morning hours of one day and the dawn of the next (the circular structure being reinforced by the division into twelve chapters). It is July 25, Festival of Santiago (patron saint of Spain), and the mixture of the religious and the secular, typical of Spanish life and literature, is beautifully intertwined throughout the novel.

Conceived from the "inside," the narrative fittingly begins in the hotel room where the two matadors are awakening to the day and death. The opening lines are a dream monologue of Rafa, *"el Filigranas"* ("The Delicate"), the younger of the two, within whose words some of the major motifs of the novel are presented in a counterbalance of fear and hope: Abundio Hernández, *"el Aceituno"* (Rafa's assistant), fear of the horns, past lives of great matadors, blood, riches for his mother and sisters, death, glory in Madrid, a lovely blond girl, sex. It ends with the leitmotif of the flies buzzing around his head, which throughout the work are symbolic of the churning, buzzing sensation of fear and repressed passions. There is an ironic contrast between the dreams of glory and the reality of their surroundings—a sordid room with cobwebs on the ceiling, rusty iron beds, and, on the dirty white walls, faded religious figures surrounded by splotches of blood. (This latter red-white color motif is consistently linked with the thematic structure of the work, that of blood sacrifice.) It is a negative, alien environment which contributes to the isolation and fear of the two matadors, who present a contrast between themselves.

Rafa, only twenty years old, is thin and pale, the personification of illusion and innocence. His name is a reference to the Archangel Raphael (associated with light), and there are also Christ-like images that will be reinforced during the course of the novel. But the character is not developed, and it is Abundio Hernández who, surprisingly even to the author himself,[7] evolves as the true protagonist. Heras calls him the "first great creation of Lera,"[8] and another critic has termed him "one of the most convincing literary personalities of the contemporary Spanish novel."[9] Nicknamed *"el Aceituno"* ("the Olive"), he is dark-complexioned with negroid features, and although only thirty years old, is wasted by failure, hunger, and fear: *"I lost my courage*.[10] . . . I wanted to be a matador, but I was not able. I had more fear than hunger, in spite of the fact that I almost never had a warm meal" (316). The underlined phrase is repeated several times by Aceituno, and is the key to the tragic concept of the character and the novel—the "tragic flaw" in each that keeps them from being whole. A gypsy foretold that he would receive as a trophy the ears and tail of a black bull, but he is unbelieving as he is only Rafa's assistant, accompanying him as a favor to his employer. Outside in the streets, the fated bull is being chased by a group of youths. Their leader is Colas, *"el Raposo"* ("the Fox"), a "youth" of thirty-five. He is a primitive being, full of dignity and charisma, dominated by a blind passion for Fina, the village prostitute. Similar to the picaresque heroes and representative of the Celtiberic roots of the nation, he is a strange mixture of barbarity and nobility—capable of the greatest brutalities and of the most sublime traits of loyalty and companionship.

In the town tavern, the public reaction to the two bullfighters, mistaking Aceituno for Rafa, is prophetic, for as in an hourglass, the two will change positions within the course of the novel/day, and as Rafa and Aceituno later walk toward the center of town, the people appear to gaze in curiosity at the "outsiders." The camera focuses inside the houses of the leading townspeople, who are presented to the reader by a combination of dialogue, interior monologue, and the observations of the people in the street. Lera's major characters seldom dominate the work, allowing the secondary ones to stand out—each one illustrating a fundamental aspect of this microcosm of provincial society. Antonio Iglesias Laguna observes that "they are archetypical characters, that show the great powers of observation of the author."[11]

Ramón, the mayor, with his innate nobility, austere dignity, and courteous manners (all evidenced in his formal attire), is the perfect model of the rural political boss. His wife Antonia, a matronly figure, aids him in the dressing ritual which will later be echoed in the preparations of the other characters and the bullfighters themselves. They are discussing the unhappiness of their daughter Antoñita (a young, blonde version of her bourgeoise mother), whose fiancé, Juanito, has renewed his visits to Fina. As the procession passes below in the street, Antoñita is on the balcony, and there is a fatalistic exchange of admiring glances between her and Rafa.

Juanito's father, Don Juan, is an example of the rural doctor who, as representative of the "black Spain" theory, not only must contend with a lack of instruments and of modern scientific knowledge, but also with the forces of superstition and tradition, symbolized by the oppressive heat and his equally oppressive wife. His isolation and sense of frustration and fear are skillfully captured by the author as the scene is characterized by his profuse perspiring (showing concern over the fate of the matadors), and his futile attempts to open the window. The shadow of his failure is his son Juanito, who, although studying medicine, is the prototype of the ineffective dandy.

Juanito had been the cause of Fina's present situation, as his having abandoned her in Madrid resulted in her being brought back to the village as a prostitute for the use of wealthier men. Her continuing relations with him are motivated by a desire for revenge, and she provides a link among el Raposo, Rafa, and Aceituno (similar to the structural function of Mercedes in *The Forgotten Ones*). She is described as "overripe," with a mixture of the sensuality and goodness associated with the Mary Magdalene types found in several of Lera's novels. As the procession passes by, Fina, strangely attracted to Rafa (hope of salvation), prepares her silken white sheets and red mattress for an anticipated later meeting with the matador, and prays before her altar. The scene, a red and white mixture of passion and purity, is associated with the preparation for the bullfight, as both rituals are a confrontation of antagonists (man/woman, man/bull) in which there is a sacrifice symbolized by the letting of blood, and in which the successful overcoming of death allows the freedom of renewal.

The final events of the morning constitute a reinforcement of the above images, via a juxtaposition of the church bells and the bellowing of the bull—the Mass and the civil ceremonies accompanying the beginning of the festival. And the ritual of sacrifice that is to come (here the bullfight) is seen in the preparations of the townspeople; a mixture of red and white colors, pungent odors, and piercing sounds—"the horns of fear": "The street already smelled of poorly cooked rotten meat, whose bitter aromas were escaping from the kitchens. . . . Rare were the doorways or corrals where one didn't see bird feathers or bloody animal skins stretched out in the sun. And all this because the previous night had been a Saint Bartholomew's massacre of the corrals. . . . The thousand agonies of the animals, with their shouts and screeches, were the announcement of the fiesta" (370).

At high noon (Chapter 4) the glaring, stultifying atmosphere is reflected in the conversations of the men in the tavern, who saturate themselves in a gluttony of food and drink and talk of women. Against this background is seen the contrasting restraint of Rafa and el Raposo, whose loyalty is shown in his benevolent camaraderie with the bullfighters and his supporting statement: "You fight without fear, I'll be there in case anything happens" (382). Returning to their hotel room, Rafa and Aceituno talk in order to ward off sleep, and the resulting scene, with technical varieties of reverie, flashback, and dialogue, is psychologically astute. The thoughts of both, triggered by the conversation, reveal the past that led them to their present situation. A reference to Aceituno's job as a bootblack triggers a flashback that manifests the subservient humiliation of the job, appropriate to his appearance and present state of mind. Later Rafa tells him of the death of his father, his interrupted doctoral studies, and the inspiration of Manolete,[12] who "began more impoverished than [himself] . . . and in a short time he became a millionaire. . . . He didn't have an extraordinary brain like Einstein or like García Lorca. He was, simply, a man like me, like you, like all of us" (391). The myth is humanized, embodied in recent years in the figure of "El Cordobés,"[13] and it is this hope that impels youths like Rafa to gamble all or nothing in an attempt to escape their poverty. But although Aceituno, like Manolete, truly had a talent for the bullfight, he had failed to reach the top, and was back at the bottom of the ladder. And Rafa, although skilled, does not have the vocation. Here are seen the ironies of life (one of the main themes of the novel) and the necessity of beginning again.

In spite of Rafa's optimism, Aceituno is not convinced. He paints an ugly picture of what lies ahead, and the word "fear," like a "black bird," hovers fatalistically over the room. It is a Cain/Abel, black/white tension as Aceituno attempts to leave, and the resulting struggle ends with his choking hands around Rafa's throat. Layers and layers of self-deception have been stripped away until there is nothing but naked reality, the middle point of the hourglass where both figures are equalized. The cowardly attacks of Aceituno, his following solicitous care over the body of Rafa, and the arrival of el Raposo are foreshadowings of what is to come. And the exchanging of positions, the second section of the hourglass, begins with Rafa's succumbing to terror and tears, as Aceituno urges him to continue. The poverty of the dressing ritual (sweat-stained and ill-fitting garments lacking in splendor and adornment, which are a pathetic covering for their nakedness and fear) is in keeping with the tragically grotesque climactic event. The narration of the bullfight itself covers three chapters (6, 7, and 8), and the accompanying fear is presented in its three physiological and psychological phases: the suspense, the terror, and the aftermath (all having been previewed in the previous scene, and corresponding to the structure of the novel as a whole).

At the Plaza Mayor, a note of contrast and release is provided by the appearance of two men from Madrid, a reporter and a novelist (the two professional sides of the author, evocative of Alfred Hitchcock's cameo appearances in his movies). The dialogue between the two emphasizes the classic quality of the bullfighters and the primitiveness of the situation. ("What a pair! . . . Don't they remind you of Zuloaga? The black man presents a stupendous image! . . . Yes, I'm reminded of Goya and Solana too. There is something tragic and grotesque here" (422). The tragic element is inherent in the bullfight itself, and in the situation of the two matadors previously described. The grotesque element appears in the improvised bull-ring, the terrified bull, the absence of picadors, and inexperienced matador, as well as the drunken musician whose trumpet note is a deformed, wobbling note ("the horns of fear," which in its English translation, gives the word "horns" an appropriate double meaning). But the scene does not fall into deformity and there is an admirable balance of opposites, as seen in the contrasting abandon of the town and the restraint of the matadors. Above all, there is a synthesis of beauty and ugliness in the figure of Aceituno as he places the *banderillas* in the back of the bull. "No one saw his jaundiced eyes, nor his narrow forehead, nor the green color of his skin, nor his negroid lips . . . He was beautiful, with that upright flexible beauty of the rush and the palm" (432).

All are united in a common bond, as the reporter points out to his companion: "Now everything is full of fear. Death has entered into the plaza and no one knows where he has sat down to watch. This may seem like literature, but it is the truth. If it weren't for fear, this would not be worth the trouble. Death is who puts the salt here . . ." (432). In Spanish society, Death is accepted as a part of life, and indeed gives it its relevance and vital quality. It is the successful conquering of Death which allows release and renewal, and the matadors are the chosen "priests" for the ritual which will purge the people. The bullfighters are surrounded by the people, a complete unity of structure and content echoed in the circular plaza with its sunny and shady side: animal/man, fear/hope, death/life. They are both inspired and victimized by the crowd, whose passions, desires, frustrations, and fears are expressed through sporadic dialogue between the principal characters, and which awaits to be purged of emotions through the tragedy of the bullfight. Rafa and Aceituno are literally caught up in a vicious circle, as the crowd distracts and torments the bull, then begins to berate them for not being able to control it.

"The trumpet call to death opened the great dramatic interrogation of the afternoon. All the preparations, expenses, efforts, hopes; the long wait of a year's time, the profound excitement of the day; the firecrackers, the wine, the sun. . . . All this had only one objective: the death of the bull. That was the reason for the fiesta. There the whole town was gathered to shudder, to suffer, in order to feel death like a cold air, and afterward, to enjoy the triumph of life, as if in order to value it the town needed to meet death face to face" (435). In the climactic moment, Rafa looks up at Antoñita and is caught on the horns of the bull. Aceituno, betrayed by his fear, remains glued to the spot, and it is el Raposo, loyal to his word, who retrieves the body of Rafa from his martyrdom (the horns of the bull, symbolic of a cross). Part of the ritual of sacrifice has been completed, as "the blood oozed out between his fingers and dyed red his suit and the white shirts of the boys" (440), and the priest scurries to get his oils. But the frightened bull is still alive, the fiesta is not over, and there is still another matador to face death. Aceituno, completely alone and surrounded by a hostile crowd, is terrified and trembling, but his trajectory from horror to heroism has begun.

The confrontation (anticlimax) is a study in black, as Aceituno and the old bull are described as a single "living ball of black flesh." After a brilliant performance (described with terms and techniques which manifest the author's knowledge of the event), Aceituno approaches the dying beast on his knees, with his arms outstretched in a cross, while his thoughts constitute a confession accompanying an act of repentance. "Forgive me, Rafa, I was a coward! . . . One must have courage like I have now . . ." (450). The ritual of sacrifice is complete, as Aceituno receives his trophy, the two ears and tail of the bull prophesied by the gypsy, and rushes to the side of Rafa, who has died. The tragedy of Rafa is contrasted with the ironic victory over death by Aceituno, and thus the tragic irony, "the black beauty of the fiesta."[14]

The third stage of fear, the aftermath, is an affirmation of life as the town prepares for the evening's festivities. But the body of Rafa is still present, and the emotion of fear will be replaced by guilt in the hour glass of the day. The visiting doctor from another village, speaking for the scapegoated Don Juan (who, ironically, was the only concerned and responsible townsman), emotionally pleads their innocence of Rafa's death, seeking refuge in the doctrine of fatalism. The dirty, blood-stained body lying in the city hall (the secular power) will later be purified and placed in the cemetery chapel (the religious authority). And representatives of these two institutions rationalize their guilt in two cult-of-death orations. The secretary speaks of the "virtue of our race . . . which knows how to die well . . . it is our philosophy" (463), while the priest affirms that "his was a beautiful death. . . . He went without pain, so to speak, and comforted by the aids of our holy religion" (459). The body is then transported to the chapel, and Chapter 10 of the novel presents a reversed march through town (this time accompanied by the shadows of the evening), as again the camera focuses on the houses of Antoñita and Fina, both representative of guilt associated with sexual desire.

Antoñita, unable to forget the tragedy, bemoans her guilt. But these feelings are assuaged by her mother, whose bourgeoise preoccupation with what people will say takes precedence. When, from the balcony, they watch the funeral procession pass, both cross themselves piously. Next the camera focuses on Fina, with a jump back in time for, as the "outcast" of society, she had not been able to attend the bullfight (and, indeed, was not allowed to attend Mass). During the course of the afternoon she had perceived the events through the symbolic sounds in the distance: the shouts of the crowd (like those which demanded the crucifixion of Christ) as a background for the trumpet and the church bells (both a call to death).[14] Upon learning of Rafa's fate, she, like Antoñita, is overcome by feelings of guilt. But, unlike her middle-class counterpart, she allows her true feelings to be shown; and as the procession passes by, all are able to hear the sobs of Fina, "the only heartfelt sob that Rafael García, "el Filigranas," received on his last walk" (490).

Aceituno, as the embodiment of Everyman, is characterized by both a feeling of guilt and continuing fear. Back in the hotel room he is offered publicity and fame by the two men from Madrid and only in the final scene does he determine to go to the cemetery. His journey is punctuated by fear of the night (portrayed with images of pathetic fallacy) and of the wrath of "Raposo," as he stealthily enters the chapel and encouters Fina at the casket, covering the body of Rafa with her white sheets. The resulting love scene in the outdoors is an affirmation of life and natural instinct, but is blighted by an awareness of their sacrilege and by Aceituno's impending flight. And the feeble crowing of a cock symbolizes their guilt and fear. The theme of man's existential situation and the paradoxes of life are summed up in Aceituno's own experiences, as he says: "Life is such suffering! When I wanted to be a matador, I couldn't. And when I had forgotten about it, they send me to this town to accompany Rafa. He did have dreams. But a bull kills him. I would have wanted to flee then, but they oblige me to fight the bull. Other times I was afraid of the bull, but this time it is the bull who is afraid of me. I wanted to die and was unable. It wasn't important to me to win and I won. . . . And you, [Fina,] you were waiting for him and I came along. And here we are. Life!" (517). Yet the cock's crow also symbolizes the beginning of a new day, as Aceituno continues down the road of his life, with hands raised in salute to Fina, whose words are the last ones of the novel: "What a life!"

In *The Horns of Fear* the bullfight is seen as a sacrificial ritual combining both pagan and Christian images. The latter imagery, influenced by the strong Catholic tradition, abounds.[15] Rafa assumes a Christ-like role, somewhat weakened by the strength of Aceituno, his follower, and the connecting thread of the novel supports this theme. The linear walk from the hotel to the Plaza Mayor to the graveyard is similar to Holy Week. There is a procession from the Garden of Gethsemane, to the Cross, to the Tomb (following the persecution by both secular and religious authorities), which is reinforced by the progression of the day from light, to shadow, to dark and dawn again. There are strong touches of irony reflecting the author's anticlerical attitude, particularly with regard to repressed sexuality and superficial religious practices. The primary emphasis, however, is on the necessity for confronting the fear of death and the validity of sacrifice. Thus Rafa's death allowed Aceituno to find his inner freedom, as after his sacrifice Aceituno is moved by love to repentance, and obtains victory over himself and the bull. In turn Fina, released from her obsessive desires for revenge by the accepting love of Aceituno has the hope restored of moving on to a better life.

From another point of view Rafa and Aceituno can be viewed as two parts of a whole, representing, respectively, the idealistic and realistic aspects of man. This theme is represented structurally by the external circular form of twenty-four hours and the contrasting day and night; and by the bull-ring with its sunny and shady sides. The relationship between Rafa and Aceituno assumes the configuration of an hourglass as they exchange positions during the course of the novel/day. Despite his role as a Judas figure, Aceituno takes on strength and modernity similar to that figure in *Jesus Christ Superstar,* in which the personage of Mary Magdalene/Fina is likewise prominent, and Christ is portrayed as a sexual being. Aceituno, although rooted in the primitive tradition of "Black Spain," is complex Everyman with his burden of fear and guilt in the face of his existential situation. It is his humanity, the contradictions of his own nature complementing the exterior paradoxes of life, that makes him tragically beautiful and one of Lera's most authentic novelistic creations. Indeed, the novel itself is considered by some critics to be Lera's best creation to date, and most agree with Robles when he says that *"The Horns of Fear* is a novel, novel, novel. In other words: it contains all the necessary ingredients of the genre. There is sufficient invention, descriptions which are brief as well as precise, very authentic characters, scenes of impressive realism, a style full of naturalness, and appropriate language spoken by each one of his creatures in the circumstances in which they live. . . . It is a complete novel, closed, succinct, like a bull-ring."[16]

La Boda

Like *The Horns of Fear,* the setting of *The Wedding* is taken from memories of Lera's youth. But the plot itself was triggered by a newspaper article[17] and is related to a story by Blasco Ibáñez entitled "La cencerrada" [The Charivari].[18] The plot, briefly, is as follows. Luciano, nicknamed "the black," is a rich, widowed foreigner who, in opposition to custom, wants to marry Iluminada, the prettiest girl of the village. Opposition to the marriage is so violent that the wedding ends in a charivari (i.e., a tin-pan serenade at the door of a widower on the night of his remarriage) precipitating the death of Luciano and one of the young men of the village. It is a simple situation, but with the dramatic possibilities artfully developed. In contrast to *The Horns,* there are fewer colors, relying on a predominantly black-white scheme appropriate to the wedding ceremony. There is even greater intensity than in the former novel, the trajectory being direct and fatal, and the result of the collison of two strong wills: that of the village versus Luciano. Again, the village is characterized by a blind devotion to tradition and an abysmal ignorance of the outside world, and the protagonist is an "outsider."

Luciano is a man of great self-confidence and wide ambitions. This larger-than-life image causes him to dominate the work, relating him to Alejandro Gómez in Miguel de Unamuno's *Nada menos que todo un hombre* [Nothing Less Than a Man]. His somewhat ostentatious show of wealth and power as well as his extreme good looks arouse the envy and even the hatred of some of the townspeople. He has returned to this village to make his home near his brother José, the schoolmaster. And although Luciano is very generous, as manifested by the provisions he makes for his future bride and her family, his greed and insensitivity to others' feelings are the flaws in his character which lead to the final tragedy.

The Prelude opens appropriately in the early morning hours of a fall day, corresponding to the age of Luciano, who is in his middle years. He is joined by Iluminada's father, Tomás, a wizened old man who agrees to "sell" his daughter, and arrangements are started for the marriage to be held the following summer on the night of the Festival of Saint John.[19] The setting is a wooded spot that is to be the site of Luciano's new home, and from which can be seen the steeple of the church. The two symbols of the pine tree and the steeple are towering and rigid, reflecting the unbending nature of the town in both their secular and religious traditions. The pine tree is related to the economy of the village, based on the selling of timber from sections of pine groves which are divided among the townspeople. Ironically, ownership of the groves is held by the women of the village, thus the prohibition against women marrying an outsider. Further restriction on freedom of choice is implied by the church steeple, as a widower is not allowed to marry a virgin.

Luciano, although wealthy enough to compensate the town financially for the loss of the pine grove, and an excellent mate for Iluminada, will be opposed by an irrational and unbending town. This opposition is represented by the Pelocabra clan which includes the father and his sons Isabelo and Margarito. The old man gave his sons feminine names because he had wanted daughters, and this seeming confusion of sexual identity is one of the major themes of the novel. Isabelo has left home, and as such represents the freedom of civilization versus the barbarity of the village, represented by Margarito. The latter figure, who appears at a distance in this scene, is described thus by Tomás: "He always walks alone through the mountains, like a wolf. He doesn't care for his father's sheep nor for anything. He's only good for cutting wood, but his hatchet is the best, that's true" (528).[20] Margarito is a rejected suitor of

Iluminada, and the above images of the wolf and the hatchet link him not only with the barbaric nature of the village, but also with the violence that will be directed at Luciano. The passing train ends the scene, adding a further ominous note, as Isabelo, a former sweetheart of Iluminada, is expected to return to defend the honor of the clan. This latter leitmotif runs throughout the novel as a connecting link as well as a hope for modernity and change which Isabelo also represents.

The remainder of this section of the novel introduces us to the other major characters, beginning with Tomás's family. His wife, Venancia, wears a black shawl, characteristic of the dress of provincial women imposed by a state of continual mourning, and as such, constituting indirect social criticism by the author. As in the Pelocabra family, her son Venancio has her name, emphasizing the somewhat unhealthy closeness between mother and son in a male-dominated society. The main focus, however, is on Iluminada. A quiet girl of inner beauty and strength, she is similar to other heroines of Lera who are not only outwardly beautiful, but capable of asserting their wills in matters of love. Although she exemplifies the subordinate and obedient position of women, in the presence of Luciano she becomes "illuminated," and he too appears to be rejuvenated. The images of light and hope reflected in these two principal characters are echoed in the dedication of the novel which reads: "To María Luisa, my wife, because she illumined the hope in me" (5).

An account of Luciano's past given to his bride reveals that although his name had not been drawn in the lottery for the war in Africa, he had sold himself for eighty *duros,* enabling his father to buy an orchard, and went as a soldier in place of another. Not wanting to return to the poverty of his village after the war, he decided to travel to Portuguese Angola. There he worked hard and established a small store, later adding a café with gambling tables. The majority of his earnings was sent home to his parents, who later died, and to his brother José. While in Angola, Luciano met and married Milagros, a young Andalusian dancer, but soon after, she was attacked by a drunken Portuguese and died. Taking justice into his own hands, Luciano killed the assassin with his rifle, and later sold his store.

Returning to Spain and his brother's home, Luciano encountered his sister-in-law Rosa. A beautiful but shrewish woman, her disillusionment stems, in part, from her marriage, and the appearance of her brother-in-law arouses in her a sexual desire and envy echoed in the other women of the town. Attempting to seduce Luciano, she falsely accuses Iluminada of having had an affair with Isabelo. This motif of supposedly lost honor, later repeated by Margarito, is a principal one in the tragedy and links it to Spanish tradition as well as to Shakespeare's *Othello*. Luciano brutally repels her, but tortured by desire he dreams of his first night with Milagros, his former wife: "He looks at her without speaking, feeling that his eyes are filled with woman, as when at night the moon fills all the sky. . . . He takes her in his arms and runs with his prize who is dripping pure water from the lake and who smells like a night bursting with the fragrance of the white rose" (556). The images of purity associated with the first night ritual will later be related to Iluminada. The stain of lost honor that hung over the first marriage is reminiscent of Pérez de Ayala's *Tigre Juan* [John the Tiger] and *El curandero de su honra* [The Restorer of Her Honor]. And the continual juxtaposition of past and present by means of flashback adds to the theme of fatality.

The dominating theme of the marriage night ritual is continued in Chapter 1, which occurs on the day of the wedding, as Luciano and José converse in the nuptial bedroom of the completed house. The contrast between the two men is seen in the joy and enthusiasm of the elder brother as opposed to the characteristic apathy of the younger, repeating the dialectic of will versus resignation found in the other novels. Their conversation serves to underscore the indomitable will and resulting blindness of Luciano in the face of the environment and traditions of the village, with which José as schoolmaster has had to contend. "Here they frown upon everything that is not traditional. . . . For them it is a matter of honor" (563). The contrasting leitmotif of the train is reiterated, now associated with Luciano's drive for wealth and power, and he reveals to José his fear of poverty, which links him to the protagonists of *Horns*; "as the train was leaving and I was losing sight of Mother, who was crying, I said to myself: 'Until I am rich, I won't return. Until I am rich, I won't return'" (562). José pleads with his brother to leave after the ceremony to avoid the charivari. But the first night is an obsession with Luciano: "I have always dreamed what this night should be . . . after the first time when I couldn't do it this way" (569), and he prophetically displays the rifle he had used to kill the assassin of Milagros.

The second section occurs in the village plaza, involving everyone in the preparations for the wedding and in the air of impending tragedy. It begins and ends with a derogatory song being spread abroad by Margarito, and the villagers become a type of Greek chorus providing background to the theme. A group of young men are constructing a wine fountain for the festivities, and a group of young women are gathered around the water fountain. The symbolism of the wine versus the water suggests the biblical wedding at Cana, but because of repressed passions, the wine becomes a means to drunkenness and violence rather than a joyful celebration. Sexual envy is expressed by both the men and the women, and speculations as to the arrival of Isabelo by train adds to the sense of impending conflict and violence.

In the following section involving Iluminada and her mother, the elegance of the nuptial site is echoed in the gifts of jewels, perfume, and silken clothes that Luciano has given to his bride. But Iluminada, in contrast to her fiancé, manifests fear at the anticipated encounter between the latter and Isabelo, as Venancia, in the manner of Pepe, serves as the warning voice of the village. Again the first night theme is introduced as the daughter affirms her virginity and is given instructions by her mother: "We all shout . . . the blood is the important thing . . . we must shout at its loss. . . . The blood is the most important thing for the men on the first night" (591).

The drama of the blood ritual is reiterated as Venancia envisions a gathering of the older women at the post-nuptial bed. "The house is inundated with light, a hazy light. . . . Black shoes and slippers, black cotton stockings, black skirts, black shawls. Dark hands folded over their stomachs; their heads hooded. . . . There are mouths without teeth and mouths with blackened teeth; stupid eyes and vicious eyes; narrow lips and lips latticed with wrinkles" (596). In a juxtaposition of light and dark, the mysterious female figures take on a Goyaesque air of mystery and witchcraft as they form a chorus that witnesses the Pagan/ Christian ritual of bloodshed with its accompanying shout, and red and white images corresponding to those in *Horns*. "They group around the matrimonial bed, where the wrinkled bedclothes show the vague forms of those who lay on them. . . . There is something like a fainting caused by religious emotion. . . . Venancia symbolically throws back the sheet. And then there is a small shout, an emotion that envelops them all. . . . 'And she was honorable!' " (597).

This scene, which points up not only the sexual fears and superstitions of the older women but also the generation gap between mother and daughter, ends with the arrival of Ricarda, Iluminada's only friend. She represents the enslaved condition of women as well as the sexual frustration of the girls, whose choices for marriage are limited to the village youths and who are often condemned to spinsterhood or the convent. This frustration is echoed in the males, as we later see the lone figure of Margarito chopping down a pine tree, his frantic hatchet blows providing the only outlet for pent-up violence and frustration. Margarito is reminded by his father that he is cutting trees in alien territory, an action later related to his invasion of the sanctuary of Luciano's home, but he defends himself by voicing the theme of clan honor. His real motives, however, are betrayed by his moaning the name of Iluminada. The closing phrase, "What astuteness!" repeated several times by Pelocabra, leaves a note of fatality and tension hanging in the air.

This scene leads naturally to the following: the gathering of the men at the village barber's, another hatchet symbol. For the "astuteness" of Margarito is that, on the pretext of honor, he will involve the entire town in his obsessive desire for Iluminada. The masculine atmosphere is appropriately characterized by crude, suggestive dialogue and humor, and the mounting tension is reflected by the comparison with animals in heat. Ironically, however, the shaving ritual here is associated with a Samsonian demasculinization, and is fittingly executed by the fat barber Albino, a pathetic figure, whose nickname, *Escaso* ("Lacking") implies not only a lack of beard, but also of male genitals. His escape in wine, his frustrations vented on the face of his tormentors, and his wielding of the razor are prophetic of the role he will play in the surprise ending.

This theme of confused sexuality is related to the following scene where Luciano, approaching his brother's house, is observed from the balcony by Rosa. Her words emphasize the mixture of good and evil in the inhabitants of the village: "It's not that they are bad. At heart they are noble and full of integrity. But the fact is that they have an exaggerated sense of masculinity" (622). This dialectic is personified in the figure of Rosa herself, who, because of her frustration and envy, is a shrewish wife and malicious gossiper, but who is conscious of her faults.

Her final burst of passion and anger directed at Luciano is contrasted with the self-effacing and unselfish love of her maid Mariana who has secretly provided for Luciano's sexual needs. Both women represent rather typical responses of many of Lera's characters and point up the injustices of the double standard.

As is characteristic of Lera's style, the final scene constitutes a synthesis of the entire chapter. Here the technique of simultaneous narration is unified by the sound of the train, complementing the atmosphere of heat and tension that continues through the noon meal. The camera focuses in turn on various segments of the village, then on Iluminada and Luciano. A group of youths are seen preparing a strange sack; three old men passing a *bota* of wine voice opposition to the outsider, while Iluminada is appropriately silent. Only Luciano continues to be optimistic: "This is my last meal as a bachelor. . . . Today is, without a doubt, the biggest day of my life. . . . I believe that it is now when I am going to begin truly to live" (664).

The dressing ritual, similar to the matadors' preparations in *Horns,* occupies two sections involving Iluminada and Luciano, respectively, with the accompanying element of the village chorus divided into its two components. The men gather at the open door, symbolic of their freedom, while the women bring to reality the previous reverie of Venancia. In an artful combination of tone, dialogue, and gestures, they emphasize the eternal preoccupations of the Spanish provincial women dressed in black: sexual fears and superstitions, painful childbirth, and death: "Here we are never able to take off our mourning clothes" (653). The appearance of Iluminada is the high point of the scene, as the myth becomes personified: "Iluminada was the myth. The myth that walked and moved like a shadow. . . . 'She looks like the Virgin!' " (661). The picture is completed by the last gift of Luciano to his bride. The gift, ironically presented by the abandoned Mariana, is a bunch of artificial white gardenias. And the dialectic of the ideal and the real is resolved in favor of the latter as Iluminada is dizzily twirled about by the villagers: "The vaporous and intangible myth, upon discerning the weakness of the flesh, turned out to be a woman" (663).

The return to reality is carried over to the next section, which begins with a flashback in Luciano's mind to his first wedding, and its contrasting black and white colors. "In the small missionary chapel a black priest had just said Mass, aided by a black acolyte. Both of their faces shone and they seemed blacker next to the starched whiteness of the liturgical clothes" (664). The ceremony is interrupted by the bizarre figure of a moustached man with riding boots and whip who voices the theme of lost honor and who resembles the seducer of Angélica in Casona's *La dama del alba* [The Lady of the Dawn]: "I have bought her many nights for less money than you, you shitty Spaniard" (665). The spell is broken, and the last words of Luciano—"Don't cry anymore!"—are echoed by Milagros and will be repeated in the final scene of the novel. Returning from his reverie, Luciano tears up the picture of Milagros, signifying a break with the past, and dons the traditional black wedding suit with contrasting white shirt. This color motif, which dominates the novel, corresponds to the past versus present, despair versus hope, underlining the dialectics of the novel.

The wedding ceremony, accompanied by the music of the *Ave María,* and witnessed by the villagers, is interrupted only briefly by the ominous note of the train whistle. In the celebration that follows, there is drinking from the wine fountain, noises of the firecrackers and musicians, and the jubilant dancing of the young people. These group scenes are some of Lera's best, in which he is able to capture not only the noise and color, but also the underlying tone. In this case the underlying tone is one of impending violence, and an intensity which has been slowly but steadily mounting. The scene is not unlike that in *The Godfather,* [21] in which violence is being plotted behind the scenes, almost making a mockery of the marriage ceremony itself. Thus as the townspeople depart there are prophetic close-ups of three groups of figures: the drunk Escaso; two youths from another village who have been tied to the wine fountain; and Margarito and his followers bearing heavy poles.

The arrival at this point of Isabelo is not only anticlimactic but a silent and unexpected one, for he came by truck instead of by train. The reader's suspicion that he is not the instrument of the honor vengeance is confirmed by his ignorance of the day's events. His encounter with Margarito is punctuated by the latter's breaking of the plaza lights, and is symbolic of the Cain/Abel tension between the two brothers as well as between the forces of stagnation and change. Isabelo represents the freedom and enlightenment of the city versus the enslavement and ignorance of the village, an ironic reminder that the barbarism of the villagers is not past history, but a present anachronism in juxtaposition with the outside world. The conversation between the two reveals the cause of Margarito's obsession as he laments: "Every night you used to tell me about how you were making it with Iluminada. And then I wasn't able to sleep" (698). Isabelo accepts the burden of guilt resulting from his own exaggerated "machismo" and false bragging, and reiterates the necessity for sexual freedom and broader horizons beyond the village. Yet the wheels of violence have been set in motion and the novel hurries toward its final climax and conclusion.

In a brief moment of calm, the bride and groom walk through the woods toward their home. But the door to the house has been symbolically boarded up, and lying on the bed is the drunken figure of the impotent Escaso. The marriage is consummated and Iluminada's virginity confirmed, but the newly-weds wait in fear of the anticipated charivari. Tensions are released by the sounds of fighting cats and dogs set loose from gunny sacks, and Luciano, enraged by the obscene chantings of the youths, shoots his rifle into the air as a warning, setting off a rapid flashback to his earlier shooting of Milagros's assassin. The theme of fatalism is reiterated as Luciano remarks: "Each one is born with his destiny. It is like a mark for all of life. Mine is a bad, twisted destiny. For that reason I have had to fight against it without ceasing. . . . I don't know, but I feel at times as if a hand were grabbing me by the neck in order to drown me in the waters" (737).

Until now there have been no zigzags in the plot, but in the climax there is an unexpected turn of events. The jeers and challenges of the young males demand that Luciano defend his honor, and he is confronted boldly by Margarito in hand-to-hand combat. But the protagonist is suddenly stabbed in the back by the drunken Escaso. Thus the most manly is defeated by the least manly, and the rifle goes off, wounding Margarito, the victim of his own plot. With the aid of Iluminada, Luciano returns to the fortress of the bedroom as the reactions of the townspeople are recorded. Isabelo, carrying a knife presented to him by Pelocabra, arrives at the plaza and encounters the bragging Escaso, simultaneously executioner and victim of the town's frustration and envy. Hurrying to the house he encounters the bleeding Margarito, and thereby forced against his will to defend the honor of the clan, enters the bedroom to face the rifle of Luciano. Iluminada, however, again assumes the role of Virgin as she intercedes for the life of her former sweetheart, and so Isabelo escapes to carry away the dying Margarito. The final scene unifies all the previous themes, with emphasis on the relationship between love and death and the ritual of sacrifice and renewal. The action occurs in the following sequence: the despair of the two lovers in the face of Luciano's impending death (a result of the stabbing); a final reenactment of the sexual union; the death of Luciano; the presence of the female chorus; and the hopeful ending.

The confrontation with death, and the temporary reprieve from it, causes Luciano to remark: "Now is when I see how truly beautiful life is" (750). Furthermore, his desire for a final sexual union is related to a man's obsession with sex as a release for his fear and anxiety. The drive to repress the awareness of death falls with particular weight not only on the "macho" of Spanish culture, but on Western man in general because of his reliance on the "myth of potency."[22] Iluminada's role in the ritual emerges in her earlier confrontation with Rosa as she manifests a hidden passion and strength: "Luciano is mine! Do you understand? Mine!" And in the final sex act she embodies the myth of Mother Earth who devours her own: "She is killing him.—Who?—She, Iluminada . . ." (754). For the Italian *amore/mortes* ("love/death") connection in myth and literature also has its biological analogies in nature. As Sigmund Freud points out: "This accounts for the likeness of the condition of that following complete sexual satisfaction with dying, and for the fact that death coincides with the act of copulation in lower animals. These creatures die in the act of reproduction because, after Eros has been eliminated through the process of satisfaction, the death instinct has a free hand for accomplishing its purpose."[23]

The tragedy, as in Greek drama, occurs offstage and is communicated by cries and the voices of the female chorus. It is accurate, as Rollo May points out, in the sense that the daimonic does occur in our lives generally slightly offstage, i.e., in the subconscious and unconscious.[24] The realization of the daimonic frees Luciano from morbid ties to the past, specifically the ties to his mother and first wife, Milagros. And the villagers, as witnesses, are "cleansed with pity and terror," as Aristotle put it. The redemptive essence of the drama appears in the role of

Iluminada, who, after being sacrificed to Luciano's desire, is now a young widow. But there is hope for the birth of a child, and the last words of the novel juxtapose the humble love of Mariana (related to Fina in *Horns*) and the dawn call to Mass (related to the cock crow in *Horns*):[25] "Only Mariana remained with her eyes open, without blinking. . . . Outside the birds of the forest were awakening and the little church bell was ringing joyfully for the dawn mass" (755).

Based in reality but involving universal myth, and structured to the dramatic unities, this novelised drama is both classic and modern. *The Wedding* is also written in the line of Spanish tradition and includes the major themes of the Golden Age drama: religion, tradition, and the conflict of wills moved by honor[26] and love. Because of these themes and the rural setting, the association with García Lorca's *Bodas de sangre* [Blood Wedding] is inevitable. Present in both works are a primitive, rural society; an atavistic cult to inherited custom; an atmosphere of violence and hatred; a misinterpreted concept of honor; a bloody fight over a wedding that involves two families; death on the wedding day; and the use of a chorus. But Lera's characters are of flesh and blood rather than expressionistic abstractions, and the devastating results of machismo are further emphasized in *The Wedding*. The feminine names given to men, the physical similarities of Isabelo to his mother, and the overly idealized position of mother, sister, and the Virgin point up the underlying weakness of the macho.[27] Thus the device of having Escaso commit the crime of honor is both grotesque and ironic. The main focus, however, is on the barbaric cruelty of the village and the fatalistic greed for power of Luciano—the same opposing forces as in Rudyard Kipling's great adventure story *The Man Who Would Be King*. As in *Horns*, a strong note of tragic irony underscores the author's often fatalistic attitude toward the possibilities for change and renewal. This attitude, however strong in these two novels given their rural setting and the novelist's own personal situation at the time of writing, will be ameliorated in the subsequent novels.

Chapter Six
Summer Storm
and The Trap

From the rural setting of the two previous novels, the author returns to Madrid. The themes of hunger and materialism in postwar Madrid as described by Cela in *La colmena* [The Beehive] are present here, but modified, for the year is 1960 and conditions have changed. The basic hunger drive has been somewhat ameliorated and general prosperity is apparent. In like manner, the decline of Catholic morality and the influence of foreigners have led to greater overt sexual freedom. But it is a hypocritical situation, for behind the outer illusion of economic progress is a reality based on opportunism, corruption, and influential connections. And behind the illusion of progress in human sexual relations are not only the hypocritical vestiges of associated guilt feelings and the double standard, but also a commercialism of sex that is both sordid and dehumanizing. The tone of the novel *Bochorno* [Summer Storm] underscores a frantic grasping for the "good life" (Lera terms it the "fourth dimension")[1] that leads to misplaced values and a moral and spiritual void.

Written from a middle-class perspective, the novel focuses on a typical family. The father, don Luis, a bank lawyer, is a man of high moral courage and a deeply felt sense of duty and responsibility. But, although strong physically, he is emotionally fatigued and spiritually disillusioned. His matronly wife, Pilar, is still very attractive, and as a helpmate to her husband she struggles to sustain her family's needs in the face of a growing inflation. But the pressure to maintain status is shown in her desire for the yearly vacation, a new maid, new clothes, etc. By contrast, their daughter Piluca, a more worldly-wise and cynical version of her mother, rebels against the middle-class obsession with form and appearance.

The protagonist of the novel is Miguel, a law student at the University of Madrid who represents one aspect of the rebellious generation of the 1960s. As a young adult, becoming aware of the discrepancy between the ideals and education of the home and school and the realities of his environment, he comments: "Our parents are good . . . but life is not as they blindly insist on believing that it is. As soon as we leave home and see and hear what occurs and is said in the streets, we realize that something is a lie: either the home or the outside world" (888).[2] The book is dedicated to Lera's own children, Angel and Adelaida (who were ages nine and two, respectively), in the hope that "when you are old enough to read and understand the following pages, the problems found in them will have evolved to the point where you will already be living their reasonable and humanistic solution." In the dedication, Lera distinguishes between two types of youths: "arrogant and angry youths," and "normal youths." The former group are "the result of a negative posture, apathetic and impotent, . . . but who never were, nor are, nor will ever be revolutionaries." The latter form the majority and are the "dark and compact force which push man toward his destiny. They suffer and cry, but they work." And it is this latter group which is the focus of the novel.

The time of the action is May, and the heat and tensions of the impending exams are portrayed in a university scene where the defects and hypocrisy of the educational system are given voice by the author.[3] The juxtaposition of the old and new is underscored by the appearance of tonsured priests dressed in black who are ill at ease among the young women students. The dialectic of past and present and the themes of the hermeticism of Spain and deceptive appearances are revealed in the conversations of the students: "Iberian snails, that's what we are. Iberian snails stretched out in the African sun. . . . We don't have a theater, a novel, or a movie. . . . How are we going to have them in this hypocritical atmosphere?" (873). As reflected in the title, *Summer Storm* (signifying repressed passions and conflicts on the verge of eruption), the principal theme of the novel is crisis: the crisis of Spain in the mid-twentieth century, clinging to medieval traditions while seeking to enter the modern industrial world, and encountering the evils of that world; the crisis of youth caught between the ideals of their parents and the realities of the environment; and the crisis of the individual in search of his identity.

This crisis is centered in the figure of Miguel and shared by his peer group at the university, particularly by his girl friend Cristina. Their conversations revolve around the generation gap and the problems of communication with their parents. As Miguel observes: "When I'm out on the street . . . I almost feel sorry for my father. He seems to be living outside of reality. . . . But when I am at his side and I hear him speak serenely, and I see him full of integrity, I feel so safe and happy, that I would like to embrace him joyfully" (853). The relationship between father and son is a beautiful one of mutual love and respect, the cornerstone of the novel. Home and its ideals (as opposed to the realities of the outside world) are represented by Luis's den, where the two always meet. Although symbolic of the love and moral teaching of the home and of the father's dedication to his work, it is also related to the middle-class emphasis on academic titles and the professions—a burden that falls heavily on the son. Luis as a bank lawyer has become involved with a wealthy businessman named Leandro. The latter, like "Moneywad" of *The Forgotten Ones,* is representative of those opportunists who, although of poor origins, became rich after the Civil War. Portrayed as a man of constant activity, his flamboyant life and flexible morals collide with the gray life-style and rigid morals of Luis, producing one of the main dialectics of the novel.

Both father and son are tempted by the lure of the outside world, and the double motifs of money and sex involve both characters, uniting them in a common plot:

Salazar, a friend and colleague of Luis, has come under the influence of Leandro and owes him a lot of money. As payment, Leandro is using Salazar as a means of obtaining the support of Luis, who is responsible for providing financial reports on those seeking substantial loans from the bank. Both Salazar and Leandro attempt to involve Miguel in their plan by suggesting that they will be able to help his father earn more money. Thus they introduce Miguel to Leandro's beautiful blonde secretary, Merche, who succeeds in seducing the naive Miguel. Luis, too, succumbs to temptation, agreeing to write a false financial report for Leandro. The structure of the novel complements the central theme, crisis caused by the confrontation with temptation, with Miguel as the pivot, corresponding to the symbol of crisis, a point within a circle. The circular image is reinforced by the division into thirteen chapters, with the last chapter being the beginning of a new cycle. related to the spiral of growth and evolution and corresponding to the emerging maturity of Miguel. As previously stated, the crisis of Miguel is extended to his family, his peer group, and to society, represented by his relationships with his father, his girl friend Cristina, and the prostitute Merche, respectively. Rhythmic interplay of these relationships allows the author to make observations of Madrid society from several points of view.

In the dialogues between father and son, the theme of fantasy versus reality and false appearances is poetically invoked by Luis's nostalgic reminiscence over Miguel's childhood confusion of linnets and sparrows. The climax of their relationship comes in Chapter 12 as Miguel, disgusted at his affair with Merche, seeks solace with his father. Luis, in turn, reveals to his son that he has promised to write a good report for Leandro. The mutual confession and recognition of the dialectic between good and evil in the human soul have a purging effect on both. As in the case of Rafa and Aceituno in *The Horns of Fear,* there is a reversal of roles, as it is Miguel who now sets the standard for moral courage and urges his father to continue the fight.

The symbolic destruction of the report on Leandro signifies a new beginning and Miguel's maturity. This new freedom is again emphasized in the dialogue between Luis and Pilar that takes place against the background of a TV soap opera (related to the theme of evasion of reality). Luis asks: "How can you expect them to ask us advice if we do nothing but tell them fantasies? . . . I don't know if it is our fault, but we can do nothing for them now. Absolutely nothing!" (945).

Miguel's relationship with Cristina is symbolized by a tree on the Avenida de Menéndez y Pelayo, the meeting-place where they have pledged loyalty to each other. Cristina's parents, however, want her to spend a year studying in America before marrying, and the pressures of waiting are reflected in group scenes of their peers where the temptations of the fast life, the easy money, and premarital sex appear. At a modern café, representing the lure of materialism, the author spotlights the two figures of Alejandro and Manolo. The former, dressed in expensive clothes, always has money to spend. It is implied that he is involved in the selling of pornographic literature. Manolo, a contrasting figure, has broken off relations with his girl friend Luz because of tensions resulting from the repression of their mutual passion. He is an alter-ego of Miguel, and their conversations, reiterating the leitmotifs of sex and money, represent a vicious circle corresponding to the structure of the novel: "—We need a mattress.—And for that we need some money.—It is a vicious circle from which there is no exit. I don't know what good youth is. Youth, youth! Just one more lie!" (788).

The theme of sexual repression is further emphasized in a gathering of the young people in the home of Pacita. The girl's parents are stereotypes of those who are preoccupied with their own interests, leaving their children to their own devices. But the author is successful in capturing the atmosphere of food, drinking, and the loud music of the prerock era. The central ideal of the section is the distortion of sex resulting from hypocritical repression and guilt. And as one of the boys points out: ". . . here there is abstinence, chastity belts, and severe punishment. . . . But let's not be hypocrites; here also one gets away with what he can, but on the sly, obviously. . . . If the movie houses, the banks of the river, and the bullfight stands could talk" (806). Sharing a mutual anguish of containment, Miguel and Cristina remain chaste. Manolo, however, confesses to Miguel that he and Luz had succumbed to their passion, and now there is no turning back for them. The emphasis is on the feelings of fear and guilt that accompany their sexual relations, the understood lack of contraceptives (illegal in Spain), and the inevitability of pregnancy.

Manolo, realizing that marriage at this point would mean the end to his university studies and his hope for a career, asks Miguel if there is no other solution. The latter, voicing the words of the author, replies: ". . . for us, no. It seems to me that the problem is different from fifty years ago, but the solution is the same" (889). Irony inheres in the fact that Miguel and Cristina had barely escaped a similar fate, and that Miguel's "solution" is to have an affair with the high-class call-girl Merche. These fallings from a rigid moral stance are further revealed in the figure of Cristina, who in desperation tells Miguel that she will not go to America as her father wishes and that she will do anything that Miguel desires. Yet, as in the case of Miguel's confrontation with his father, he sees reflected in Cristina his own weakness, and together they determine to support each other and to do what is right in their own eyes.

Merche, together with Leandro, embodies a corrupt society and the carpe-diem philosophy associated with excessive sex and money. Yet she, like Fina, is also the stereotype of the whore with heart who suffers the tragedy of falling in love. The expensive nightclub they visit together underscores the atmosphere of commercialized sex and unhealthy sentimentalism stimulated by low lights, alcohol, and lachrimose music. The dialectic of appearance versus reality and its accompanying disillusionment is further reinforced by the unexpected appearance of Piluca. As the older brother, Miguel's initial reaction is one of fury, but he realizes the hypocrisy of his protests. The theme of false honor is accentuated by Merche's demand for a kiss ("As if I were a decent sweetheart" [924]) and the melodramatic tone of the scene is carried over to their arrival at an expensive restaurant. Disillusionment results as Miguel meets Alejandro, his well-dressed peer, in the company of a notorious homosexual. The tension is broken when Miguel bursts into hysterical laughter and later sobs in the privacy of his room: "It was a night of vice, of dirty sex; a night of nightmares and fears; a night of storm and of shame" (931). His final confrontation with Merche is a melodramatic scene in which the violence and sordidness associated with her are revealed in her having been brutally beaten by Leandro. She has one moment of sweet revenge and hope when she realizes that Luis will not write the report for Leandro and that the latter will be ruined financially. But her violent hatred for Leandro and her equally passionate affirmation of love for Miguel are contrasted with the painful disillusionment and compassion of the protagonist.

The plot lines of the novel, in the figure of Miguel, depict the existential themes of loneliness, limit-situations, and the necessity for choice. During the course of action his growing self-awareness and identification with others result in the recognition of good and evil, courage and despair, within himself, in those closest to him, and in society itself. But freedom is achieved through his confronting directly the various crises in his development, moving from dependence to greater maturity and higher integration by relation to the world around him through creative work and love.

As a social novel, *Bochorno* can be criticized from two points of view: validity at the time of publication, and its present applicability. In 1960 the book was a controversial success, and as Lera commented: "*Summer Storm* is a very controversial novel and that pleases me. The polemic means that I have touched the wound of present-day society."[4] In some respects it can be considered a forerunner of subsequent literature and actualities. Many of the themes—materialism, commercialized sex, human corruptibility, and manipulation of others for personal gain—are today universally recognized and common preoccupations; and Lera foresaw the present realities of the so-called generation-gap, resulting primarily from hypocrisy in the home and in education.

Having been myself a student in Madrid during the year 1962 permits me to attest to Lera's successful portrayal of student life, which, in Madrid (and in Europe in general), is a "street life" as compared to the previous "car life" and present "apartment life" of American students. Dating consisted of walking and sitting in outdoor cafés and bars, money allowing, with moments of privacy relegated to darkened doorways of the Plaza de Toros, a situation contributing to the desire for money and to the disproportionate allure and feelings of guilt associated with sex. Due to economic necessity, most students lived at home, and family contact was maintained, if only at the traditional evening meal.

The author has posed many questions that have still greater relevance today: Can the youth be blamed if they do not desire the life of their middle-class parents, whose goals of respectability are so closely related to the acquisition of a new car or television set, and who, disillusioned and exhausted from their treadmill existence, place the burden of their frustrated lives on their children? The strong bonds of affection and friendship between father and son described in the novel were rare in the 1960s. More usual were the strained silences or, at best, mundane and trivial conversations that covered up the real and underlying concerns and crises of the young people. Only maturity on the part of both—father and son—allowed such a relationship. But how can youth find themselves when prolonged adolescence and financial dependence on the family—a result of the educational system—are the rule? We are learning that prolonged book-learning is not necessarily education, that experience is needed as a perspective if this knowledge is to become a vital part of the student. By protecting their children from the evils of society, are parents not only protecting them from the very experiences necessary for growth and maturity?

The themes of the novel have become very topical and much wider in scope, compounded not only by freer sexual mores, but by the widespread use of drugs, and Spain is no longer excluded (e.g., the colony at Torremolinos, so vividly portrayed by James Michener in *The Drifters*). Viewed from the perspective of the present, the novel is too limited thematically and too mild in tone. Although Miguel is representative of "normal youths," the opposing figure of Alejandro is an extreme case, having little relationship with "the angry youth" of later years. The latter, in some cases, are indeed closer to the true revolutionary spirit of Lera himself. The problems are no longer simply defined as money and sex and have reached greater "crisis" proportions, leading to a renewed concern with the basic questions of existence and the individual's particular role in the drama. There is a search for a less hypocritical social morality, for deeper spiritual values, more meaningful life-styles, and for better man-woman relationships that can pave the way for universal understanding.

The author's solution of "the same as fifty years ago" is certainly applicable to the universal and timeless necessity for self-discipline and knowledge, and responsibility toward oneself and one's fellow man. But the means to that end are disputable. Perhaps one may not agree with the optimism of Charles Reich's *Greening of America,* but the challenges are great and noble. We cannot forge new leaders on old anvils, and Lera himself, in a subsequent article, has demonstrated his faith in the possibilities.

"The students . . . threw themselves into action because of a saturation of nonconformity and of irritability with the spectacle of an outdated and repressive university, and because of a technological and consumer society brutalized by the satisfying of the elemental necessities. Theirs was a return to man himself—the end and not the means—and his ethical and intellectual values. It was a return to their neo-romantic character. Thus also their irrepressible force of influence. . . ."[5] From a technical standpoint, the novel possesses unity of form and content, excellent portrayal of group scenes, and good secondary characters. But there is a tendency to melodrama, and too much reliance on the confession situation instead of other introspection techniques that would be more appropriate for characters experiencing self-discovery. These deficiencies are accentuated in the following novel, *Trampa*.

Trampa

Continuing his examination of Madrid society in the novel *Trampa* [The Trap], the author now focuses on the upper class, where the search for happiness leads to a "dolce vita" existence resulting in alcoholism, suicide, or insanity. Unfortunately, the vision is myopic and the result, for the most part, is a social novel ridden with clichés and stereotyped characters. Among these is a group of young men and women, who, having no occupations, frantically attempt to relieve their boredom by partying. The central figure in the group is an elegant blonde woman named Elena, the protagonist of the novel. Her father, Germán, the typical wealthy businessman with a series of mistresses, is always absent from home. His name is associated with the earlier idealism of the war years, but his hypocrisy is revealed by his present life and his ostentatious participation in religious processions. His wife, Gracia, the stereotyped upper-class woman of leisure, is characterized by an ignorance of the world around her, and, virtually deserted by her husband, seeks refuge in a pious attitude. Her preoccupation with her charitable activities is evocative of similar Galdosian characters, and underlines the theme of religious hypocrisy: "Charity is love . . . and not giving sweaters with scorn and alms with ostentation" (1127).[6]

Yet within these two nuclei of the upper class—the peer group and the family—representing both generations, there are two interesting figures who have a special relationship with Elena, and through whom the protagonist gains profundity: Joaquín, her former lover, and Mario, her younger brother. An example of the dialectic of "apathy versus will" found in the other novels (Antonio and Jesús of *The Forgotten Ones,* Aceituno and Rafa of *The Horns of Fear,* and José and Luciano of *The Wedding*), and the dialectic within Lera himself, they are, nevertheless, related thematically. The theme they represent, that of a call to conscience, linking the social aspects of the novel (rich versus poor) with the moral and ethical (guilt and the necessity for sacrifice and atonement), is voiced by Mario: "Our pride makes us believe that God is always on our side. And that is not possible, because we are not good. . . . All those calamities of which one speaks so lightly, like nuclear war, communism, etc., may be a call to our conscience so that we may be better, and perhaps, the announcement of our penitence, of our expiation" (1132).

Joaquín the pessimist, whose "eyes, when he spoke, reflected his habitual sadness" (1074), is an echo of the note of fatality that predominates in Lera's works. Lacking hope and faith in the future, he submerges himself in the life of the group. Yet he truly loves Elena, even though he did not have the courage to marry her. Mario, by contrast, had wanted to enter a monastery, but obeying the wishes of his father had obtained an engineering degree and is now working in a factory. Caught between the two classes, he, like Miguel of *Summer Storm,* is struggling for identity and purpose: "My friends think that I am addle-brained and even worse. And other people believe, at times, that I am trying to deceive them. At first they didn't trust me, and although they are beginning to trust me more, they consider me a loner. And Papa . . . to him I am a revolutionary and a mystic, and above all a renegade who is not content to owe everything to him. And what I am looking for is the truth and to lead my own life: come on, grant me that!" (1126).

In keeping with the emphasis on the degeneracy of the upper class, the plot involves the problem of homosexuality, represented by Alvaro, Elena's husband. Related to Alejandro in *Summer Storm,* he is ironically described as the prototypical "macho"—extremely handsome, athletic, and adored by the women. Not only is the stereotype a generally false one, however, but the novel manifests a lack of knowledge and sympathy with the problem, which, indeed, is circumvented, as Alvaro is approached largely through his influence on Elena. This evasion on the part of the author is explained by Heras, who says that "Lera . . . because of his character, because of his strong masculinity, and his balanced sexuality, is repelled by the turbidness which surrounds the homosexual. He feels a true repugnance for homosexual relations, he who has created almost prototypical masculine and female characters whose sexual relations are full of a natural beauty. He has an impulsive character that can never fall into sensuality. And the treatment of the homosexual theme necessitates an understanding of the sensual."[7] Alvaro's deviation is not revealed until the end of the novel, although this knowledge is necessary for an appreciation of character development. Yet most readers will suspect it from the first chapter, and as a result the plot is overly long and superfluous. This having been said, however, the novel is saved to some extent by the figure of Elena, as she is observed in a crisis situation, her abnormal obsession with Alvaro, which leads to a physical, mental, and spiritual decline. Although lacking the close correspondence between form and content that characterizes Lera's other novels, there is a continuity between chapters. The action covers an approximately fifteen-week period, corresponding to the number of chapters and to the length of the proposed honeymoon, and extending from December to Holy Week—an ironic reinforcement of the theme of religious hypocrisy that runs throughout the novel.

Chapter 1 takes place in a hotel room where Elena is preparing for the first night with Alvaro. The scene emphasizes the themes of narcissism, materialism, and sensualism, as Elena dons a red and black lace negligee that serves as a leitmotif to the plot. Alvaro later appears, and they share their first and last sexual night together. This failure is foreshadowed by Elena's eating breakfast alone, as Alvaro, echoing the earlier narcissism of Elena, admires himself in the mirror and exercises on the balcony, an image evocative of the play *El Cuerpo* [The Body] by Lauro Olmo. Chapter 2 is set against the background of a speeding car with rock-and-roll music blaring from the radio, underscoring the theme of escape and the philosophy of carpe diem. Elena's negative reaction to her husband's conversation reveals that she knows very little about him. Indeed she had only married him for his wealth and good looks and because Joaquín's refusal to marry her. It is obviously a rebound situation whose tragic consequences are foreshadowed in the last scene of the chapter as Alvaro becomes drunk on cognac. His excuse for not making love to her, his disgust at her affair with Joaquín, is a contradiction of his earlier assurances to the contrary. And the dissillusionment and abrupt changes in personality are extended to Chapter 3, whose action takes place a month later when Elena arrives without Alvaro at a gathering of the group. Pretending happiness, she announces that she is pregnant (an improbability which is one of the weaknesses of the plot), but later at home she has the maid prepare her tranquilizers as she enters her husband's den.

The extreme masculinity of the room is contrasted with Elena's morbid sensualism, and Alvaro himself as in Chapter 5 we see Alvaro in a nightclub with two prostitutes. In keeping with the author's conception of the homosexual as existing in a "twilight zone" (neither male nor female), he is described as being "high, but without really being drunk, although he was entering the intermediate zone between light and shadow" (1040). The reader becomes aware of his self-hate and its cause as he exclaims: "Foxes, dollars, bastards, me. . . . What a repertoire" (1040). "What we were lacking at the party: a queer" (1043). These "hints" are reinforced by the reference to the Portal (a well-known gay bar in Madrid), and Alvaro's scorn of the abandoned prostitutes.

Chapter 7, the midpoint of the novel, related in structure, tone, and theme to the final chapter, presents a confrontation between Elena and Alvaro. Here Elena laments that "It's a lot to put up with being married and not having a husband, in spite of living under the same roof. I have put up with everything in silence. I have suffered alone, and day after day I have gotten drunk on those damn pills which deaden me so that I won't have to bother you. . . . All because I believe that having a child, after all that has happened between us, is well worth it" (1069). But the mention of the child, the hope for their marriage, sends Alvaro into a rage as he uncovers this hatred and the underlying vanity and egotism of Elena. "Can't you understand that my life is also a hell? I hate you and I hate myself and everyone. . . . You console yourself with the thought of a child. And what about me? My desperation is not important to you, because you are no more than stomach and vanity" (1071). Again there is an abrupt change in tone as he begs her to have an abortion, promising that he will buy the best physician possible.

This image of an impasse, or trap, is repeated in a chance confrontation between Joaquín and Alvaro, and the inevitable fight between the two. Alvaro, however, shows mercy toward the weaker Joaquín, who recognizes that Alvaro's violence is directed against himself, an expression of his own self-hatred, and that he had been contemplating suicide. Thus there is irony in Joaquín's having saved Alvaro and his assurance that the latter is the father of the expected child. The decline and desperation of Alvaro is paralleled in Chapter 9 as Elena searches frantically through her belongings for the red and black negligee of her wedding night. Its disappearance is linked to the arrival of a perfumed letter for Alvaro. An obvious plant, it is signed by "Manoli," who becomes the focus of Elena's obsession until the climax of the novel.

Her new determination to win Alvaro at whatever cost is further reflected in a scene with her mother, Gracia. The dialogue serves to point up the differences between the two generations, the passivity of

the mother as opposed to the passion of the daughter, and the contrasting reactions of both in a similar crisis situation. Against the background of Gracia's accounts of her charitable activities, she speaks of the
consolation of prayer. But Elena, lacking sympathy for the pious escape
in a superficial religion, reminds her mother that "You were thinking of
becoming a nun when you met Daddy. Later, you lived happily for
many years, without worries, with a loyal husband and with children
who adored you. And when the hour of testing came, what did you do?
The easiest thing: you resigned yourself. . . . My God, how wrong you
were! So Daddy has gone from flower to flower. What else could a sane
man who is still young do? You threw him into the arms of other
women" (1115).

Elena's contrasting passion and vow that she will lower herself, no
matter how far, in order to attract Alvaro signals the beginning of her
descent and is ironically juxtaposed to her praying the rosary with her
mother. Later, in Chapter 11, comes the revelation of a less superficial
facet of Elena's character, which up until now has been rather two-
dimensional. This new depth is revealed in her warm and close relationship with her brother Mario, who resembles her physically but who
reveals in his posture and comportment the restraint and discipline of
an interior torment. He tells her of his decision to go to Germany:
"Only in a strange country, without friends nor supporters, can one
repay the debt. I am going so that no one nor anything can stop me from
paying" (1132). The themes of guilt and atonement will later be
applicable to Elena, and Mario, in the role of redeeming martyr, prays
to share his sister's burden. She does not as yet understand, but her
following statement is prophetic of the last lines of the novel: "We
women see things in a different way. . . . We cry and wait and hope.
And we are so insistent that God ends up listening to us."

The image of supplication is expanded in Chapter 11, one of the
better chapters of the novel, as Elena walks barefoot through the rain in
a Holy Week procession. The scene is evocative of a similar one in *La
Regenta* [The Regents Wife], as both Ana Ozores and Elena are frustrated sexually and emotionally, tend toward extreme sensualism and
hysteria, are members of the upper class, which the author tends to
criticize, and manifest a feeling of superiority and aloofness from the
crowds around them.

Despite a rather stereotyped juxtaposition of the loudspeakers and the words of the priest (similar to the example of superficial religion in Goytisolo's *Fin de Fiesta* [End of Celebration], the author is successful in capturing the increasing social and self-awareness of Elena as her aloofness is shattered in the leveling force of the procession, which puts her in contact with the lower classes of society. Although she has come to bargain for Alvaro, she is brought to shame by the poverty and suffering of her fellow penitents.

Continuing the dialectic of the novel, this religious scene contrasts with the following chapter, which takes place in a nightclub where Elena and Joaquín are dancing. Joaquín promises to arrange a meeting with Manoli, and seeks to make love to Elena. Refusing him, she reiterates the theme of her fatal passion and obsession with Alvaro: "It is like a sickness . . . his odor stays on my skin . . . his voice, his look, his walk" (1169). Joaquin vows to wait for her, but this sacrificial love is juxtaposed to the following scene between Alvaro and Elena where she, failing to seduce her husband, becomes desperate as she begs to be his mistress. The melodramatic confrontation ends with Alvaro's returning to the den, the music of the record player drowning out the moans of Elena, who lies outside the door. Chapter 14 fittingly reveals Elena's rapid deterioration as in an eerie monologue she constructs in her mind the forthcoming interview with Manoli, how she will pay to learn the arts of her profession, and how afterward she will seek revenge against Alvaro by spurning his advances.

More than a picture of the female who masochistically responds to mistreatment, it is the portrayal of a woman scorned, and as Heras points out, ". . . it is love, but self-love. The self-love of a woman who sees herself dispossessed of her condition, one who not only doesn't attract, but who repels her husband. Alvaro is only an instrument, the mirror where she wants to see her femininity reflected, her sexuality which has been annulled by the greatest scorn; the indifference and insensibility with regard to her womanhood."[8] An air of incipient insanity about her contradicts her protestations to the contrary, leading up to the second section of the chapter, the climax of the novel. Joaquín, according to his promise, takes Elena to see Manoli. The meeting, arranged by his uncle, takes place in a residence outside the city. Arriving at the house, they are greeted at the door by a man dressed in the red and black negligee. Behind him can be heard the voice of Alvaro calling: "Greta! Gretita!" and Elena flees in horror.

The grotesque contract of the costumes of the previous party with the hooded figure of a Holy Week procession alludes to the title and the theme of hypocrisy, here related to Elena's father, Germán, who participates in both the party and the penitential procession and who will figure in the last chapter of the novel. The passing of the image of the captive Christ is related to Elena's preoccupation with her child and the theme of sacrifice and atonement that characterizes the remainder of the novel. The final chapter, 15, a complement to chapter 7, contains the anticipated violent anticlimax and the final confrontation between Elena and Alvaro. In a scene of mutual hate and desperation, Alvaro reveals his motive for marrying Elena: "You were the most beautiful woman I had known and you had sexual experience. Only you were able to save me. For that reason I married you" (1190). Acquiring a certain nobility in his self-hatred, he pleads with her to kill him, and the shots of the pistol are appropriately drowned out by the music of the phonograph.

Elena phones her father, who is annoyed at her call, as he is on his way to the Holy Week procession. His black hood and mask, also associated with death and the executioner, are related to Germán's subsequent arrival and accompanying of his daughter to the police station. Her disheveled appearance reflects her total decline, and Germán, certain that he can buy her freedom, tells her the lies she must repeat to save herself. But in the final lines of the novel, Elena tells the police that she killed him because he was "too beautiful." Thus purged by her confession, she ultimately achieves nobility in her role as woman and mother as "with her hands over her stomach as if to protect it. Elena sat down to wait" (1202).

In conclusion, *Trampa,* similar to *Bochorno,* presents a background of social and moral protest set against Madrid society, and the plot is concerned with a search for identity and an existential crisis situation ending on a ray of hope (the birth of the child in this case). The ethical theme of true love and charity also ends with hope as Joaquín waits at the jail for Elena, and Mario has begun his pilgrimage to Germany. But the tendency in the first novel toward an oversimplification of complex psychosociological problems and melodrama in the plot is compounded in *Trampa*. There is a lack of unity between form and content and a looseness in construction that are uncharacteristic of Lera's other novels. The technique, lacking diversity, fails principally because, as in *Bochorno,* deeper introspection is needed in keeping with the complex themes and the emphasis on the evolving self-awareness of the protagonist. The weakness of the novel, which Lera himself recognizes,[9] is a lack of firsthand acquaintance with the milieu portrayed, although his subsequent associations with members of the upper class have amplified his perspective. Yet, in fairness to the author, few novelists have been successful in portraying the upper class, and those few have, in most cases, been members of that class themselves (e.g., Manuel Halcón in Spain and F. Scott Fitzgerald in America).

Chapter Seven

We Have Lost the Sun
and A Land to Die In

Hemos perdido el sol

The figure of Mario in *The Trap,* led by his conscience to follow the emigration to Germany, is connected with this novel, *Hemos perdido el sol* [We Have Lost the Sun]. The result of Lera's own visit to Germany, it is complemented by a later nonfictional work entitled *Con la maleta al hombro* [With My Knapsack on My Back],[1] whose chapter headings contain the major themes of this novel: "Why?"—The economic, social, and political situation in Spain that forces many Spaniards to leave home; "The Wall of Glass"—The language and cultural barriers, racial discrimination, and the separation from families and familiar surroundings; "The Great Discovery"—The sanctity and creativity of work, and its unifying power which tears down class barriers; "Neither Here Nor There"—The dilemma of the Spaniards who are caught between the two cultures and the accompanying dialectic of materialistic versus humanistic values; "Woman, Love, and Death"—The encountering of a different morality, different male/female relationships, and a different philosophical attitude toward life and death; "The Landscape Inside and Out"—Germany as seen through its landscape, cities, and people; and "The Sweetheart of Berlin"—The paradoxes of the German nation and its past history of fanaticism, both symbolized by the enigmatic figure of the one-eyed Nefretiti.

At the beginning of the emigration movement, there were many seemingly insurmountable problems, including poor organization and bureaucratic red tape, substandard living conditions for the workers, lack of interpreters, and criminality on the part of a few opportunistic Spaniards. These and other problems are revealed in the novel, but at the time of the action, 1962, conditions have improved and many of the difficulties are being resolved through the mutual cooperation of both nations. I myself lived in Germany (Cologne) in 1964, and my husband worked in a tractor factory along with the emigrant workers. Personal experiences and comments, where appropriate, will be included in the notes of this chapter.

The novel begins on a train, a leitmotif representing Destiny, Time, and Change. Traveling from Spain to Germany are a group of emigrants whose lives will be drastically altered by exposure to another culture, and who, through the confrontation with this crisis situation, will experience growth and self-knowledge. Among those passengers is a young middle-class couple from Madrid, Ramón and Paulina, who have been forced to emigrate because of low wages and lack of living quarters in Spain. Newly employed by the Pluto Metalworks in Germany, they will work on an assembly line, although both are capable of more intellectually demanding occupations. Ramon is thirty years old and, like Pepe of *The Forgotten Ones,* embodies the theme of imprisoned potential thwarted by the environment. Paulina, an attractive young woman with an underlying passion, is a protected figure who has never been separated from her parents and who has known no man except her husband.

Like many couples, they have been forced to leave their son, four-year-old Ramoncito, in Spain with his grandparents. And the thread of nostalgia and pathos connected with separation is reinforced by the unexpected bureaucratic mix-up that has destined Paulina for southern Munich and Ramón for northern Hamburg. This device allows the author to contrast both regions of Germany, and to place both male and female in an existential situation of solitude and crisis. Emphasis is placed on the language and cultural barriers that give the Spaniards a helpless and childlike quality appropriate to the theme of emerging self-awareness, while a note of disillusionment and despair runs as a light thread through the novel. Yet the courage of Ramón and Paulina, characteristic of all Lera's principal characters, is echoed in other Spanish emigrants who demonstrate their tenacity and determination in the face of adverse circumstances.

Accordingly, the summer sun will gradually give way to bleak winter days, as the weather registers with pathetic fallacy the struggle against depression and homesickness of those who "have lost the sun."

The novel is divided into ten chapters. The first and last employ the leitmotif of the train station, and the intervening eight roughly correspond to the eight months of the plot duration. The alternating focus on Hamburg and Munich follows the respective actions of the two protagonists and expands to include those persons who form a nucleus around them. Each of these characters is carefully developed, and the numerous subplots are artfully integrated with the central plot.

The opening scene in Hamburg captures succinctly the atmosphere of the factory: the huge dining hall with the odors of potatoes and beer; the deafening noise of the work area; and the overall air of efficiency and cleanliness. Against this background is contrasted the group of Spaniards who are adjusting to the new environment and to a daily routine which leads from factory to dormitory, the only diversion being an occasional beer in a local restaurant.[2] The contrast of Spaniard/German is exemplified in Ramón and his work partner Hans, who has invited the naive protagonist to a party that seems to him nothing more than an orgy of drunkenness. He is further confused by the open, amorous advances of his hostess, and the seeming indifference of Hans, who is portrayed as a foolish and ineffective figure. Unfortunately the author appears too preoccupied with the question of sexual freedom, and although throughout the novel he defends the difference in the moral code, this prejudice colors most of the important German characters. Thus this scene, which is authentic but not necessarily typical, is juxtaposed with a later one involving a Spanish couple, Antonio and Catalina, who in the privacy of their shabby rented room talk of their forthcoming child and the joy of being reunited after a long separation. Having adapted readily to the environment, they are representative of those who will remain in Germany, and the pillow-talk scene is a convincing one, portrayed with tenderness and humor. Their conversation, however, also reflects the problem of discrimination that results in the barring of foreign workers from many restaurants, and the unjust association of the Spaniards with all other Mediterranean peoples.[3]

This theme leads to the figure of Professor Walter, who teaches the German language to the few Spaniards who take advantage of the free classes.[4] As the only intellectual in the novel, he assumes the role of objective spokesman for the German nation and culture, seeking to elucidate the enigma of Nefretiti. His discussion of racism and Nazism reflects the author's preoccupation with these themes, which appear throughout the work. Yet his bilingualism allows him to straddle both cultures (voice of the omniscient author), and he emphasizes the necessity for adaptability and involvement. The professor's concern for the Spaniards leads to the final scene of the chapter, which takes place in the men's dormitory, a counterpoint to the factory of the opening scene. Further delineation of the nucleus of figures around Ramón reveals each character as representing an attitude or reaction to the environment with the resulting homesickness and sexual frustration.

Rafa, the youngest of the group and having no family ties in Spain, is searching for a German sweetheart and will eventually make his home in Germany. Eduardo, small and nervous, is a rather cynical figure who has a wife at home, but who has found a Spanish prostitute who fulfills his needs. He is linked by nostalgia, symbolized by the radio with Lucio, a taciturn man, who, remaining faithful to his wife and three children, represents those who are tied irrevocably to Spain. The humorous element is provided by Jalisco, a minor character but one of the most memorable. The scapegoat of the group, he speaks with a strong Galician accent and is characterized by his wild stories and even wilder antics. Ramón, as the natural leader of the group, is a true friend to each, and his position with regard to the crisis is that of adaptability and the confronting of reality. Yet he, in connection with Paulina and the main plot line, also embodies the elements of mutability and searching, symbolized by the leitmotif of the train.

Chapter 3 focuses on Paulina in Munich one month later. The weather is ominously colder. She is in the office of a priest, Father Laureano of the Fathers of Charity, an organization which, together with the Spanish consulate, bears the impossible burden of aiding the emigrants with their personal and economic problems. Here she encounters the contrasting figure of Luis, "the Photogenic." Representative of the opportunistic Spaniards without scruples who lure women into a modern version of the white slave trade, his activities underline the theme of corruption in a materialistic society. In a factory scene corresponding to that of the previous chapter, Paulina is spotlighted by the attentive eyes of the chief of her department, a handsome bachelor of thirty named George Schneider. Confused as Ramón was by new sexual mores, she seeks refuge in thoughts of her husband and child. These passages, which provide necessary background on the protagonists, are some of the best of the novel, written with a depth of understanding and a universality that strike a responsive chord in the reader.

Continuing the counterpoint of the previous chapter, the dormitory scene focuses on Paulina's roommates, and these female characters, like their male counterparts, represent various reactions to the crisis. Fé, "a girl of shadowy coloring, tiny and sensitive, is a daughter of the sun and the steppes" (291).[5] She is in love with Karl, "a Bavarian youth, blonde like Munich beer, who is square, slow, and a son of the forests and the cold" (291). She plans to marry him in June and constitutes a thematic parallel to Rafa. Amparo, a good but self-righteous country woman, spends the weekends with her Spanish husband, who is working in another factory. Related to Luis of the Hamburg section, her children are in Spain and she plans to return when they have saved enough money. Regina, who is the thematic counterpart to Eduardo, is over thirty-five, but still vivacious and attractive. One of the most interesting female figures, she has a husband (a "lazy and cowardly man" [125]) and two children in Spain, who never write although she sends them most of her monthly paycheck. Overcome by loneliness, she is having an affair with Gonzalo, who is described as "a mature man, with a tired look, and with deep wrinkles on his forehead and cheeks" (132).

The last section of the chapter ends with this couple. Gonzalo, who has many affinities with the author, is the balancing contrast to Luis, "the Photogenic," and the relationship between the two provides one of the major subplots of the novel. Having fought for the Republicans during the Spanish Civil War and later suffering years of imprisonment, he was then forced to witness the slow death of his wife by cancer. Although disillusioned and tormented by memories of the past, he is neither bitter nor full of self-pity. His close association with the "black pain" causes him to fear the finality and horror of death and thus to affirm life: "Everything that is happening now is nothing compared to the past. For me, Germany is a vacation. The most important thing is to wake up in the morning" (136).

Chapter 4 returns to Hamburg, where Ramón is searching for a rented room for Paulina and himself. Painfully aware of his shabby clothes and particularly his worn-out shoes, the scene is reminiscent of that in Carmen Laforet's *Nada* [Nothing] where Andrea goes to the dance and her inferiority complex colors all that she sees, causing her to exaggerate the richness and happiness of those around her. Here the strangeness of the environment, the bitter cold, and his state of mind correspond to the rejection Ramón receives from the prospective land-lords. Their refusal to accept foreigners and children underlines the modern themes of noninvolvement and discrimination. The loneliness and desire for human contact are amplified to universal proportions in a later scene in the notorious section of San Pauli. Seen through the eyes of Ramón and Rafa, it is representative of the desperate attempt of man to escape his existential condition through sensual stimulation and sex. True to the author's style, the scene is portrayed with compassion for the human condition and an affirmation of life.

The two Spaniards end up in a dance hall where each encounters his Germany destiny or nemesis. Rafa establishes relations with a young blonde girl named Barbara, and Ramón is destined to be linked with Marleen. The later, an elegantly beautiful counterpart to Georg in Munich, is a cultured and intelligent woman in her early thirties. Portrayed as an independent but lonely figure who is attracted physi-cally and emotionally to the handsome Spaniard, she quickly seduces the vulnerable Ramón.

Appropriate to the dilemma Ramón will face, his meeting with Marleen is juxtaposed thematically with Paulina's reading of his letter. As a means of introspection, the letter begins with mention of their son, the link between husband and wife, and underlines the themes of frustration and a search for self. There is a repetition of the word *esperar* with its double connotation of waiting and hoping, which is associated with Paulina as she fights bravely to keep up her spirits and to still her jealous fears for Ramón. Yet her statement that "one earns money but loses so many things" (188) is prophetic of the end of the story and related to the meaning of the title.

Paulina's involvement with Georg progresses slowly as he professes his love for her, and his interior monologue serves further to delineate Paulina's character and to point up the contrast between the German and the Spanish women. "Poor thing! One can see that she is a sweet and humble woman. . . . How happy one would be with a woman like that. Our women are beautiful, there's no doubt about that, but they have lost much of their charm. They only want their liberation. . . . My friends are not happy with wives who lead a man's life. My mother was not like that . . ." (195).

This German/Spanish contrast is amplified to nationalistic proportions in the scene between Gonzalo and Regina in near-by Nuremburg. The setting serves to underline the theme of Nazism during World War II, as Gonzalo observes: "Here the Nazi pride rose and fell. . . . I believe that without the Nazis, the Spanish Civil War would not have broken out" (198). This theory of a scapegoated Spain is represented by both Regina and Gonzalo. Her story, which describes sufferings in a Spanish prison similar to the atrocities at Dachau, points out the ironies and futilities of both wars. And Gonzalo, who fought in the Spanish Civil War, is now living in Munich (near Dachau), having been forced out of the country for which he had fought. The theme is intensified by focusing on Georg as he consumes a bottle of vodka and relates his own story, from the German point of view. He speaks of the capturing of his father by the SS, his own forced induction into the Hitler Youth Movement, the raping of his sisters during the flight after the fall of Berlin, and the subsequent death of his mother. Thus his present condition manifests the irony of a peace characterized by loneliness and bitter memories.

The isolated image of the drunken Georg ending the previous chapter is related to the opening of Chapter 6, which pictures Eduardo at the train station as he is returning to Spain, himself overcome by loneliness and despair. This chapter, the midpoint of the novel, repeats the initial leitmotif of the train and accentuates the plight of the Spaniards who are neither here nor there: "If you stay, bad, if you return, worse" (226). The dilemma is later embodied in Ramón as he walks through the beautiful Alster Center, which is described with images of elegant Nordic beauty associated with Marleen. But a note of sadness is struck, as of a child looking through the window of a candy store, and connected with the image of forbidden fruit that will be repeated in the last lines of the novel.

The fear of an overpowering passion is expressed by both the characters, and the need for security is revealed in Ramón's obsessive desire for a house of his own. Echoing the story of Luciano in *The Wedding,* it is a symbol of his escape from poverty and lost identity. This theme of alienation is reinforced by Ramón's encounter with a Spaniard who is half-crazed by fear and hunger and the inability to communicate. Eleutorio, an excellent minor figure, had spent three months working on a farm where he suffered extreme discrimination. No one spoke to him and, after working to the point of exhaustion, he was isolated alone in his room at night. (This experience corresponds to Lera's own experience of three months of solitary confinement and evokes the idea of Germany as a prison for the emigrants.) Eleutorio escaped from the farm, however, and is helped by Ramón to return to Spain.

This element of salvation is related to the subsequent Christmas Eve party in the dormitory, where an air of forced gaiety covers up an underlying loneliness and nostalgia. Rafa, not present, is at the home of Barbara, where he is received into the family and Germany. Ramón, also absent, is with Marleen, where the scene is a sadder one, as Marleen, in a state of depression and drinking a bottle of champagne, relates her story. Her Jewish father was assassinated. Her German mother died in a bombardment. She herself had been raped at age eleven. Although somewhat melodramatic, the scene rings true (reinforced by the earlier chapter of this book concerning the Civil War novels) and parallels the previous confession of Georg to Paulina. Both figures reiterate the themes of Nazism, the horrors of war, the terror of haunting memories, and the desire for escape from their existential loneliness through drink and love.

The opening scene of Chapter 7, New Year's Eve in Munich, is a repetition of the Christmas Eve party in the dormitory. The women are also festive, and there is even a note of humor in their attempt to intoxicate their German housemother so that the men can come in to serenade. This device, which points up the theme of imprisonment and hypocrisy, is a protest against the childlike treatment of the Spaniards, particularly of the women. Paulina tries unsuccessfully to reach Ramón by phone, a failure of communication that causes a decline in will-power, and at the later New Year's Eve party with Georg, the champagne and midnight ritual almost shatter her reserve.

Yet Paulina's strength and personal sacrifice are echoed in the figure of Gonzalo, who, seated in a restaurant, awaits the arrival of Luis, "the Photogenic" (166). His reverie follows the theme of war and the concept of continuing duty and obligation associated with the character: "It wasn't a question of leaving or starving, but rather of fulfilling my duty. I stayed and I still haven't finished. The truth is that we never completely finish. But if one has the will to do so . . ." (284). Under the pretext of representing a firm in Hamburg which needs cheap female labor, he astutely elicits from Luis the damaging self-evidence. Thus on New Year's Eve, alone on an icy bridge, Gonzalo knocks him out and throws him into the river. While attempting to escape, however, the car skids to a crash and the pressure of his hands on the horn is a plaintive note of pain and despair: "It was a long, piercing scream that penetrated the silent, frozen night, like a hot knife" (303). The sacrifice having been accomplished, this violent death injects a new note into the novel, as reflected in Regina's desperate attempt to reach the hospital. The cold of the night and the loneliness of Germany are echoed in the indifference of the couple who give her a ride, and in the nurse who is annoyed at being disturbed. And Gonzalo, after having confessed, so that no one else would be held accountable for his crime, "remained alone forever" (311).

Chapter 8 takes place the same night in Hamburg. The previous ritual of sacrifice and atonement on the part of Gonzalo will be repeated here in connection with the sexual act and appropriate to the rebirth of the New Year. Rafa and Barbara spend their first night in the home of her absent parents, while Ramón and Marleen make love in the snow-covered Alster Park. This latter setting, previously associated with Marleen, is symbolic of purity and light and the unity of love and death—a vision of eternity. "If the ground was white, the air was equally white. There was no sky. Only the electric lights stood out, . . . like the fading reflection of an invisible illumination. . . . There was no wind or the echo of anything. Only a pure death and a pure silence" (317). The fall from Eternity is a bitter one, prophetic of the end of the novel, as Ramón reiterates the theme of the search for self and life as a great drunkenness: "It seems that I am always drunk. I don't know what I am doing or what I ought to do. Something is missing. I feel guilty as if I were a thief. I am not happy except only in rare moments. . . . On the other hand, for nothing in the world would I go backwards" (318).

This uncertainty is amplified in the dormitory scene where Ramón laments to Lucio: "We are crucified. We have one hand nailed in Spain and the other in Germany. . . . Our feet are hanging in the air. . . . That is the worst part" (323). The sacrifice of the Spaniards is not completed and Ramón has not yet found his self or his destiny. This continuing dilemma is revealed in his inability to tell Paulina about Marleen and echoes in the return of Eduardo. The latter, unable to find inner peace in Spain, has determined to choose Germany as his home. But as Ramón reminds him: "For now this will seem to be the better choice; but in a few months you will be anxious to return to Spain again" (333). These individual problems are amplified to nationalistic proportions as the search for personal identity on the part of Ramón is extended to the search on the part of the German and Spanish nations for their collective identities and destinies. The engagement of Rafa and Barbara and the expected birth of their child suggest a fusion of the best aspects of the two nations as a possible solution, and this compromise position is explored throughout the remainder of the novel.

In a later factory scene, a meeting of the Workers' Union is held to discuss a forthcoming strike. But the freedom of collective bargaining, nonexistent in Spain, is accompanied by a cold materialism that is described by Professor Walter as he speaks of the declining birth rate because children are not wanted. And a derogatory comparison is made with the United States: "Now we have no other goal than to make money and we have made that the only indisputable value. With money we get what can be bought, but on the other hand we do without those things that have no price. It is the same program of North America" (341). Further images suggest Germany's having chosen a false course and attempting superficially to bind a festering wound; a refusal to dig to the root of the problem. This avoidance of pain is intrinsically bound up with the story of Ramón and the end of the story.

Professor Walter has aided Ramón in securing a house of his own, and although it is only a shack from the reconstruction era, it is a sign of new hope. In like manner, Antonio and Catalina plan to purchase a restaurant that will provide Spanish food and music. This fusion of the two cultures in the Spanish couple who have adapted to Germany is ideal, but the dilemma of Ramón has not been so resolved. The final two chapters emphasize the changes that have occurred in Ramón and Paulina, and the necessity for decisions to resolve the individual crises resulting from this growth.

After eight months alone, Paulina has matured. "She seems more like a complete woman, with a profound and tender look in her eyes, and with greater self-assurance in her words and gestures" (366). Conversely, Regina has become thinner and sadder after the death of Gonzalo, and her decision to return to Spain with her husband reflects a hopelessness and despair unequaled in the novel. Her departure on the train reverts again to the uniting leitmotif as Paulina is left alone once more at the station to confront her own decision. Wandering the lonely streets, her desperation leads her to Georg's apartment, where she is saved from herself by the unexpected presence of Fé and Karl, who have been using the apartment as a secret meeting place. The fear and guilt associated with sex is assuaged by Karl, who represents a more wholesome sexual morality. Although Fé has chosen her German destiny, Paulina is still tied to Spain and again determined to go to Ramón. She says, "Everyone has their road, and mine is to Hamburg, no matter what happens" (397).

In the final chapter Ramón and Marleen are in the shack she has helped to decorate. Their happiness is marred by his jealousy of her past lovers, and Marleen's lament that she cannot have a child. This sterility, associated with lost hope for a permanent union with Ramón, is in ironic contrast to Barbara, who, in opposition to Rafa, has had an abortion. Both situations infer a failure to join the two cultures, and the abortive image is echoed in the following scene at the factory where "an inhuman cry of pure humanity was heard above the noise and pierced the ears of the workers" (419).

The cry, that of Lucio, who has lost his hand in a machine, evoking Gonzalo and the sound of the horn, is an image found in the other novels (e.g., *The Horns of Fear*). Lucio's sacrifice serves to unite all the Spaniards in common protest as Ramón reiterates the previously expressed dialectic of materialism versus humanism: "At this moment nothing else is important, neither the machines, nor the work, nor the songs. . . . It is our companion who is important. His bad luck, his children, they are important, do you understand? (422). Ramón later encounters Rafa, who drunkenly moans, "They have killed it." And the words, ironically related to both the aborted child and the hand of Lucio, are applicable to all Spaniards who have come into contact with the cold German machine and have lost the sun.

The pathos of this scene is counterbalanced by the birth of Antonio's child, for whom Ramón is the godfather. But Ramón himself, although a loyal friend, has been unfaithful to both his wife and his mistress. Thus Marleen confronts him: "I don't understand why you haven't decided to reveal our love to your wife. You have promised me a hundred times. . . . You have been disloyal to her and to me" (440). Ramón has lacked the courage to make a decision, and thus the choice is made for him by default as Paulina arrives at the Hamburg train station. She later appears at the shack and silently turns over the picture of Marleen, who is left standing alone outside in the rain. The last lines of the novel contain the previously mentioned element of forbidden fruit associated with Germany: "She was very beautiful, like so many other things of this land that aren't for us" (449).

The novel presents an existential crisis situation, separation from familiar surroundings and the exposure to a new culture, which promotes change and growth, necessitating further growth. But the ending is strangely unsettling, a continuing dilemma. Paulina has matured. No longer the naive, overprotected child, she has come to better know herself and is a potentially better wife and mother. And Marleen, having found a hope for happiness, had committed herself completely. Both women were loyal and honest, but Ramón was neither. Fatalism is often an excuse for man's worst actions and a temptation to passivity. Ramón asks: "Are we really responsible for many of our acts? Isn't it destiny who waits for us whenever and wherever it wants?" (445). His decision, like that of Regina, was made by chance, in this case the arrival of Paulina. He has taken the best of Germany and plans to remain, but although he is irrevocably changed, he attempts to return to the past by reuniting with Paulina. The dilemma is still unresolved and the synthesis of the two nations has not been accomplished. Ramón is neither here nor there, and like many Spaniards has lost more than the sun.

As noted previously, I myself lived in Germany, and in my opinion the author has accurately portrayed the situation of the emigrants and artistically captured the foreigner's view of Germany, which is indeed the viewpoint of the novel. ". . . This book is in no way a novel about Germany, but rather the story of the adventures of men and women— Spaniards, workers, and emigrants—in that Republic, conceived in my imagination" (Prologue). But in seeking to be the omniscient author and to present a balanced dialectic, Lera was hampered by the brevity of his visit and his unfamiliarity with the German language. Thus the result is fated to be one-sided, and if each of the Spanish figures is portrayed as a complete and complex cosmos, the author fails to grant their German counterparts the same profundity. The view of these characters is colored by two understandable prejudices: one against Nazism, and the other against a different sexual morality. With reference to the latter, German men are not so weak nor the women so easy. Marleen fails to some extent as a novelistic creation because she is too young to have given up (and in truth was modeled after an older woman)[6] and too intelligent and cultured not to have found other outlets for her loneliness and frustrations.

Heras too finds that, with regard to the major plot theme, Lera has "remained with the topical and has not touched the root of the problem."[7] Ramon has changed dramatically and has left behind him the environment where he lived with Paulina. He is deluding himself to think that he can return to the past, for his decision was already made when he determined to love Marleen and promised to marry her. The simple fact of turning down her picture will not change the fact of her presence in his life, and the very home he lives in was prepared and inhabited by Marleen.

Yet it a very good novel. The collective scenes (dormitory, factory, San Pauli, etc.) are excellent, capturing succinctly the odors, sounds and overall atmosphere. They are rhythmically alternated with the individual plot lines, to which they are related thematically, producing an admirable balance from macrocosm to microcosm and emphasizing the element of human interrelatedness. The close unity of form and content is achieved by the outer circular structure of ten chapters, which corresponds to the theme of imprisonment and crisis, and by the intersecting line of the leitmotif (the train). This line, representative of

Time, Change, and Destiny, also corresponds to the simultaneous emerging of self-awareness and the gradual penetration of the language barrier. As in the circular bull-ring structure of *The Horns of Fear,* there is also a balanced dialectic of sun and shade. Here the alternation between Hamburg/Munich, factory/dormitory, and male/female complements the themes of the novel: Germany versus Spain, materialism versus humanism, and enslavement versus freedom. In spite of the aforementioned prejudices, the novel is an astute essay in comparative national psychology, possessing numerous passages presenting these contrasts with admirable synthesis and conciseness.

Tierra para Morir

The title of the previous novel relates to the following one, as *Tierra para Morir* [A Land to Die In] returns to Spain and depicts the other side of the emigration problem, the vacuum left in the provinces. Viewed from the focal point of Spanish culture and tradition, this novel complements the dialectics and themes of the first. "Why?"—A decadent feudalistic society, comparable to that described by William Faulkner, which forces young people to abandon their homes; "The Wall of Glass"—The lack of communication between the older and younger generations, between city and village, and ignorance that refuses to admit new ideas and change; "The Great Discovery"—The nobility of work and freedom for individuals from slavery to the barren land; "Neither Here Nor There"—The plight of the young people who can never return home to stay; "Woman, Love, and Death"—The repression of love and the enslavement of women which leads to both physical and spiritual death; "The Landscape Inside and Out"—The stifling heat and aridity of the land mirrored in equally oppressive institutions which is reflected in the frustrated lives of the villagers; and "Nefretiti"—The dangers of obsession and fanaticism exemplified by the protagonist, Claudio, and his relation to the land and tradition.

The setting, an anonymous village of Spain, is like that of *The Horns of Fear* and *The Wedding,* but there is evidence of turmoil and change brought about by the influence of outside forces. Likewise structured in ten chapters, Chapter 1, with admirable synthesis, sets the tone and introduces the principal characters and themes. The opening scene depicts the arrival, at night and on a motorcycle, of a young doctor from a neighboring village. This youthful, modern image of the man of science contrasts sharply with the town, described with images of darkness and closed doors, appropriate to the theme of stagnation and ignorance. The outsider is accompanied by Manquillo, a young man whose right arm was destroyed by a firecracker at one of the yearly fiestas. He is, ironically, one of the few in the village who can read, and serves as postman for Claudio, the village mayor and representative of secular authority. During the course of the novel he is repeatedly linked with the grotesque figure of Felix, *"el Mocoso"* ("The Worthless"), reminiscent of Benji in Faulkner's *The Sound and the Fury* and evoking a similar theme of life as "a tale told by an idiot, full of sound and fury and signifying nothing."[8] He serves as the church bell-ringer for don Benedicto, the representative of religious authority. The author's originality and accuracy lie in having the two "village idiots" (parodies of secular and religious tradition) serve as witnesses to the drama, and their rhythmic appearance serves as a link between the townspeople and becomes a leitmotif of the novel.

The reason for the doctor's intrusion is the incipient death of Paca. A victim of the fierce environment and the superstitions and taboos of the atavistic culture, her prolonged suffering and ultimate death are a microcosm of the collective fate of the entire village, which, like a Spanish *bota* or martyr, is gradually emptied of its wine/blood. Paca's husband, the mayor Claudio, is the central figure in the novel (the true protagonist is a collective one, the village), whose appearance resembles that of a biblical patriarch. As a youth he was awed by the wealth of don Javier, who owned most of the land of the region, and was in love with the latter's daughter and only child, Virtudes. Working hard as a planter, he saved his money and began to buy land of his own, but don Javier witheld his permission for the marriage. Claudio left for military duty, and when he returned he discovered that Virtudes, although she loved him, had grown tired of waiting and had married Julio, a young lawyer. Stoically accepting his loss, but determining to have the largest farm in town, he married Paca, the unattractive daughter of another rich landowner. Over the years Paca was a shadow who conceived and bore children, almost unnoticed by her husband, who labored even on Sundays and religious holidays.

An intelligent man, Claudio read the Bible in order to be able to converse with the priest, don Benedicto, and accordingly named his children Josué, Issac, and Noemí.[9] (The names are symbolic of struggle, sacrifice, and faith/hope especially, some of the major themes of the novel.) He later fought in the Civil War, but returned with the determination to buy all the available land. His obsession, blindness, and lack of compassion are reflected in his securing the largest section of land belonging to Virtudes, called *"La Cuerna"* ("The Horn"), and his seeming unawareness of the death of his mother and the suffering of his wife. Conversely, he was greatly sorrowed by the sudden death of his sons, which he blamed on heredity (the weakness of Paca), and thus Noemí became the object of his ambition, if not of his affection.

His obsession with the land, which in reality dominates him, springs from his hope for a grandson to carry on his name. But Noemí, the prettiest and richest girl in the village, and very much like her father in strength and determination, identifies with the young people who have emigrated to the cities of Spain, France, and Germany. The dialectics of imprisonment versus freedom and materialism versus humanism are synthesized in the first confrontation between father and daughter as Noemí reminds Claudio that his wealth has intimidated all prospective suitors and that she is rotting on the land. Hoping to escape, Noemí asks her friend Teresa for aid in securing a passport. The latter is representative of those who have married and put down roots in the village, but whose youth still permits them a hope for change and renewal. Both Teresa and her husband Victoriano are village schoolmasters, and the opening description of the old, deserted schoolhouse enunciates the theme of ignorance, corresponding to the initial description of the village itself in chapter one: "On the walls was suspended an old blackboard and a large map of Spain splattered with the blood of dead flies and yellowed with age" (42).[10]

In contrast, the following scene focuses on the figure of Obdulia, whose house, like that of Fina in *Horns of Fear,* is situated at the end of town. Similar to Fina, she represents the desire for escape from sexual repression, and Claudio, like Aceituno, finds release for his frustrations and fears with her. She is married, however, to Santos, a pale, thin figure similar to Rafa, and who, like Lucio of *We Have Lost the Sun,* represents those who suffer martyrdom in Germany. Obdulia, left behind with three children, is the target of Manquillo and Mocoso, who come daily to offer their sexual services under the pretext of delivering the mail. The former has ironically taken over Santo's position as village postman, and he is thus the link between the town and those who have emigrated to the cities. His crippled condition accentuates the theme of lack of communication, and the severing of family ties, while Mocoso, with his lewd looks and language, is an embodiment of the hypocrisy of the church he serves. As witnesses to the life of the village, the "odd couple" observes the arrival of a mysterious figure who calls himself Sixto Arias. He resembles Pepe of *The Forgotten Ones*, "in his brilliant dark eyes were touches of malice and irony, and next to his lips, wrinkles of astuteness" (64). He is an outside force that offers escape for Noemí when he is hired by Claudio to work in the fields.

The land, which has been plagued through the years by the violent forces of nature, is like the desert that enslaved the Israeli nation, victims of a "biblical curse" (70). Yet for Claudio the land is like a sensual woman and thus related to his frustrated love for Virtudes: "The day in which Claudio dug his spade into the tender earth of 'The Horn,' Virtudes felt within herself a deep tearing pain, as if she had been violated, even though she could not hear the savage cry of possession" (205). The younger Sixto, however, is neither so obsessed nor so sensual in his relation to the land, and he hopes to be a mechanic. This attitude is seen in his first encounter with Noemí in which he, realizing that she has never known a man, abandons his "machismo." And his friendly overtures are the first manifestations of male tenderness that she has known.

In contrast to the above scene, the Sunday sermon, delivered by the reactionary don Benedicto, concerns immorality and communism, and his authoritarian glance is directed at Sixto, who has been obliged to attend by the equally oppressive figure of Claudio. Like Noemí and the younger generation, he is caught between the horns of religious and secular tradition, the establishments of *The Horns of Fear* that caused the crucifixion of Rafa. The trinity of government, church, and school is emphasized in this chapter, the latter establishment being represented by Teresa and Victoriano. As a younger couple with a child, they suggest the possibility of education as a means of release from blind tradition, yet they themselves seem to have succumbed to apathy. The section terminates with the sound of the church bell which, described as the cry of a child, is like the "voice of one crying in the wilderness."

Chapter 4 begins with the two pairs of figures who will terminate the novel: two old men seated in the village plaza, and Manquillo and Mocoso. The earthy language of the latter pair is an ironic bravado masking their frustrated sexuality and lives. Their struggle over the privilege of delivering Santo's letter to Obdulia results in Manquillo's biting off the ear of Mocoso, which the latter grotesquely offers as a tribute of his love to Obdulia. The scene, reminiscent of a similar one in Cela's *La familia de Pascual Duarte* [The Family of Pascal Duarte], is also a paradox of the Garden of Gethsemane, where Peter cuts off the ear of the slave of the highpriest. Thus, with obvious religious overtones, Obdulia pours water over the head of Mocoso and the baptismal image is followed by a state of grace, with "a strange smile of peace, of gratefulness and love on broken and swollen lips" (123). This ironic ritual of sacrifice and redemption, a foreshadowing of the role of Santos, is interrupted by the arrival of Claudio, who orders the pair to do penance by cleaning up the village cemetery.

These latter elements of guilt and atonement are also extended to the relationships between Noemí and Sixto and that of Claudio and Obdulia. In a scene involving the younger couple, Sixto commits himself to Noemí, denying all claims to her wealth and lands. He has chosen humanism over materialism and life over death, but Noemí is still tied to her father and to stifling tradition. Wounded by Sixto's bitter sexual restraint, she departs silently "like the shadow of a punished and wounded woman" (131). The image of a shadow, related previously to her mother and symbolic of conscience, is also connected with Flora, who serves a similar function in the relationship between Claudio and her mother, Obdulia. The theme of repressed passion is repeated here, as Claudio tells her that he will not come again, and they are intrrupted by the shadowy figure of the castigating conscience in the form of Flora.

Continuing the theme of conscience, Santos returns from Germany in a scene that evokes images of the Palm Sunday entry into Jerusalem. The happy scene is appropriately juxtaposed to his incipient martyrdom as he confesses to Claudio that he had gone to Germany because he knew that he was dying of tuberculosis and was determined to sacrifice his life for his children. Now he has returned to Spain to die, and his sacrifice is contrasted with the hypocrisy of Claudio and Obdulia. Noemí's coldness toward her father is not only a result of his infidelity to her mother, but also of his corresponding mistreatment of herself. Yet she does not fear him and she challenges Sixto: "You are also afraid of my father. . . . I am a woman and I don't fear him" (153).

Chapter 5, the mid-point of the novel, provides a break in tension as Claudio departs to another province to search for planters, and his absence allows for the union of Sixto and Noemí. The latter, symbolically facing herself in a mirror, prepares a meal for herself and Sixto and goes to join him at "The Horn." The sexual ritual, a union that was not accomplished by Claudio and Virtudes, takes place in the outdoors, emphasizing the naturalness of the sex act and the equality of the partners. This section also provides further background on Noemí, Lera's strongest female character. As a child she, like her brothers, had run freely through the fields and attended school. But upon reaching puberty at the age of twelve her education was terminated, and like Cinderella she was forced to assume the heaviest household duties. The burden of the family honor, guarded with iron authority by her father and brothers, was placed on her. And the fear of sex and childbirth that caused her to spurn Julio was motivated by the suffering of her mother. Withdrawing into herself, her greatest wish was to have been born a male. This wish ironically links her with Claudio, for as Teresa points out: "Your father, in his heart, is resentful because you were not born a male. And you also. And neither of you two are to blame" (165).

Teresa, however, serves as an alter-ero to Noemí, representing the peace and fulfillment that comes from a good marriage and children, and enabling her friend to accept her femininity. Noemí's decision to love Sixto, in spite of tradition and her father's authority, frees her to be a fulfilled woman—a rare accomplishment among Lera's female characters. The mutual love and trust between her and Sixto also allow the latter to achieve inner freedom, as he reveals his real name (Agustín Lorca Arias) and his past history. He confesses that he had been forced to flee from the civil guards because of his involvement in a mining strike and the false accusations of a personal friend. (The two events are related to the themes of communism and immorality in the sermon of the priest.) He assures Noemí that he will accept responsibility for his freedom, and asserts: "I am not a vagabond. . . . I know what I have to do and I will do it" (171).

The ritual of sacrificial love is juxtaposed with its counterpoint, death (although both are related to the theme of personal commitment), as we witness the last moments of Santos. It is high noon, corresponding to the middle of the summer and the novel, and to the time of the Crucifixion. The stifling heat and the hovering of the flies, like buzzards anticipating a corpse, echo the themes of stagnation and fear found in *The Horns of Fear*. Santos's feeble attempts to ward off his tormentors are a foreshadowing of the ultimate death of the village itself. The ironic fate of Santos, who "came to die here after having traveled so far" (186), is echoed in the church bells, whose double note sounds the dialectics of the novel, and in the arrival of the women in black, who reiterate the theme of enslavement inherent in the title. The conversation of the men revolves around the motif of death, emphasizing the Spanish attitude of resignation and acceptance that paradoxically gives meaning and nobility to life. The image of a chorus gathered around the cross is similar to those scenes in *The Horns of Fear* and *The Wedding*. Here, there is a partitioning of Christ's clothes (the removal of Santos's boots), followed by total darkness as the candles are extinguished, and when the cock crows in the early morning, only Claudio is watching. His lone presence here is prophetic of the end of the novel, and the last lines of the chapter focus again on the two church bells whose notes are like "the beating wings of a crow over the village" (132). Their ominous sound evokes the well-known lines of John Donne (who, like Santos, suffered from tuberculosis) that inspired Hemingway's novel of Spain: ". . . never send to know for whom the bell tolls; it tolls for thee."[11]

Santos returned from Germany to die, but the younger generation of emigrants, represented by Virtudes's son Julio, must make other choices. His car radio jarringly disrupts the serenity of the village with a popular song of 1964 ("Give me/give me, give me/happiness that only you/can give me" (194), a leitmotif throughout the chapter, associated thematically with that of *Summer Storm*. The radio, as Julio tells Virtudes, is an escape from solitude, and he further reveals his decision to marry a Spanish girl whom he met in Germany and his plans to live in Barcelona. He hopes to take his mother with them, yet the title of *A Land to Die In* is appropriate for Virtudes, whose life, like that of Santos, is an embodiment of the title theme.

The following passages describing Virtudes are some of the best in the novel, picturing with understanding and compassion the plight of women in the provinces. "A piece of soap, water, a mirror and a comb, were the only elements of her coquetry. Her greatest luxury, a bed with two downy mattresses. She didn't know what love was, because she fell in love with one man and married another. . . . She was not yet fifty years old and she already appeared old, not in the decrepitude of her body, but in the resignation of her spirit." "No one spoke to her of anything except work, pain, harvests, weather, anguish, and fear. She always lived in the country without knowing if she were plain or beautiful, and without the temptations of looking at the stars, or the moon, or the waters of the river." "Nevertheless, she cried sometimes without asking herself why, and all her affection was poured out in kisses to her son when he was small, and in caressing looks when he was older" (204).

Virtudes, who is tied irrevocably to Spain, the land, and the past, cannot adapt to change or accept hope. And the freedom of love and new horizons related to her son and the younger generation is juxtaposed contrastingly with a meeting between her and Claudio that is characterized by pathos, painful memories, and lost opportunities. Virtudes confesses that she had been wrong in not waiting for him, and he in turn assures her that he has forgiven. She, still hopeful of a redemption for past mistakes, speaks of her cherished dream for the marriage of Julio and Noemí, which would unite the two families and "The Horn." But Claudio sees that their children will not repeat the loveless marriages of their parents, and the section ends with the beginning of Virtudes's decline.

Other families arrive from the Spanish cities to open the houses of the village temporarily and to celebrate the summer fiesta. Among them is the opportunistic Robus, nicknamed "Fart." From the same mold as "Moneywad" of *The Forgotten Ones,* and Leandro of *Summer Storm,* he comes every year to open up the bar. This establishment, with the background music of the radio and the dancing of the twist, is the scene of the collective escape of the young people. Noemí, too, escapes to Sixto's room, but the love tryst is interrupted by Claudio, who attempts to impose his authority. Sixto, frustrated by the older man's refusal to listen, is not intimidated and leaves the house. Noemí, too, defies her father's domination of her life and their confrontation here brings about

the beginning of disillusionment in Claudio, but the beginning of hope
for his daughter: "The tiredness, the terrible tiredness of a lifetime,
struck him in the chest, filled his eyes, and rose in his throat. Noemí,
however, ascended to her plenitude, stronger than ever. The sudden
confrontation with a truth to which she clung as a last hope [her love for
Sixto], redeemed her at that moment from all the timidities and fear of
a long servitude" (264).

The pathos of Claudio is further deepened by the sudden announcement that his land is on fire and the new wheat is burning.
Although he suspects Sixto, Manquillo reveals to him that the fire had
been set by Flora, her father's avenger. Virtudes later reminds Claudio
that a simple lie would place the blame on Sixto, thus preventing
Noemí's escape. But Claudio chooses truth and sanity: "You think you
are alert, but you are asleep. . . . Or do you want me to go crazy too?"
(269), and his compassion toward Sixto is repeated in his refusal to
persecute Flora. Again he goes to visit Obdulia, and the two, freed now
from their past lives and commitments, make love. But the union is
overshadowed by their previous hypocrisy and present guilt, symbolized by the chorus of cock crows.

The complete disintegration of Claudio is echoed in the following
scene in which his agent, Manquillo, seeks to molest Noemí in exchange for his knowledge of Sixto's whereabouts. She escapes from her
lewd attacker and again confronts her father in a scene similar to that of
mutual recognition between parent and child in *Summer Storm*. Noemí's
union with Sixto was consummated in freedom and light and both will
accept responsibility for their choice. She has chosen humanism and
love, and the hope for the future is represented by the child which she is
expecting. In contrast, Claudio's union with Obdulia was consummated in enslavement and darkness and they denied their choice. He
had chosen materialism over humanism and mistaken possession for
love. Aware now that he is losing everything, he seeks to drown his
sorrows in wine and forgetfulness.

There is a last desperate rise in the plot line as Claudio appears the
following day dressed in his finest clothes and with his habitual air of
self-assurance. At the Town Hall, Virtudes signs over the deed to her
remaining land, marking an end to her hope and Claudio's complete
possession of her. He dreams of replanting the land and bequeathing it

to his grandson, while retaining the title to "The Horn." Thus his future (the child) is again tied to a blind obsession with th land, both representative of man's desire for immortality. As Noemí says of him: "He believes that we are the land and nothing more. . . . For him honor is as important as life itself, but the land means even more than life and honor. And the grandson has become the land for him" (290). The air of false jubilation associated with Claudio is extended to the village as it plans for the coming fiesta. There will be no firecrackers, because of the lack of funds, and Robus is chosen to pay for the sermon. Images of poverty, darkness, and irony are synthesized in the suicide of Virtudes, who achieves freedom in death by drowning herself in a well. Overcome by remorse, Claudio closes himself in the dark barn, alone with the animals, while Julio escapes in his automobile. The anticlimactic fiesta is a sordid parody of that in *The Horns of Fear,* but in a similar manner to that novel, the religious procession passes through the streets and by the doors of the two women who because they are still in mourning are excluded from the festivities: Obdulia and Noemí. Both are young and beautiful, but enslaved by a hypocritical morality and an oppressive tradition tying them to the past and authoritarian restraints. A note of hope is associated with Noemí, as she smiles at Teresa, and the theme of the emancipation of women is repeated in the sermon of the visiting young priest. "He said that customs were changing and that the women of the villages as well as those of the cities ought to prepare themselves for greater liberty; that their personal dignity is possible only through independent and dignified work; that the times are past in which they had to be totally dependent on a man; that everything depends on their having a strong moral foundation, being unafraid, and that they become accustomed to dealing with the opposite sex in all fields and endeavors" (315). The repressive tradition is finally laid to rest, as the tearful village Virgin being carried by the men soon becomes a burden too heavy to bear, and only Claudio refuses to give in. The church bells, too, are silenced, and only one unisoned plea is voiced in Latin by the villagers: "Ora pro nobis."

In the concluding chapter, Victoriano and Teresa reaffirm their love, making plans to leave the village because "it seems that in this town everything dries up, even one's feelings" (238). Noemí has gone to France to marry Sixto, fulfilling her biblical name. Only Claudio remains alone in the fields of "The Horn." Noemí's promise to return during the vacation is linked with his new plants as Claudio stoically affirms: "Let them believe that I am as crazy as poor Virtudes. Look out friends, look out. . . . I have to live at least until these plants bear fruit" (334). And as the priest watches with him, the figure of Claudio, "nailed" to the spot, appears larger than life among the rows of empty houses. The last scene of the novel ends with the reconciliation of Manquillo and Mocoso, who walk arm and arm through the village square. The Town Hall is completely dark and even the two old men have left the plaza before the call to the rosary. The final words are fittingly those of the village idiot: "Baa Baa"—the last drop of blood from the lamb, the martyred village.

The end of the novel is rather pessimistic, suggesting the collapse of traditional secular and religious authority. Yet the lingering presence of Claudio holds out the possibility of an enlightened tradition that is flexible with the changing times and needs. Education and responsible sexual freedom (represented by Victoriano and Teresa, Sixto and Noemí, respectively) provide a key to that enlightenment. Also important is economic growth by means of creative work and the emancipation of women. Hope for the future, both of the individual and of the village, is embodied in the expected child and the newly sown plants of Claudio. The role of authority is questioned, whether that of parent over child, husband over wife, or government over nation. And the separation of church and state is advocated, although Claudio (secular) and the priest (religious) remain standing together on the land of "The Horn" (a two-pronged image related to the bull). As in the other novels, the criticism is anticlerical rather than antireligious, as seen in the enlightened sermon by the younger priest.

Stylistically speaking, there is a perfect blending of form and content that is complemented by the title. The beginning chapter image of the cemetery underlines the theme of the stagnating land and death, with emphasis on Claudio. And the final chapter repeats this image, but with a slight note of hope, characteristic of all Lera's novels, implying the beginning of another higher cycle. The intervening chapters portray a gradual depletion of the village and the old traditions, with the deaths of Santos and Virtudes occurring at rhythmic intervals. The counterpointing notes of hope and renewal are strengthened by the younger generation, who escape in pairs, in contrast to the lonely deaths of their parents. The final union and equilibrium of the village idiots complement the solitary, but sane and living, figure of Claudio. Apart from their social themes, both *We Have Lost the Sun* and *A Land to Die In* are universal in scope, making a plea for individual freedom and human understanding, with emphasis on the healing power of love and the naturalness and beauty of the sexual union. Moral responsibility is connected with this freedom of choice, and a necessity for commitment and sacrifice exists on the part of nations as well as individuals.

Chapter Eight
A Man Sells Himself

Se vende un hombre, [A Man Sells Himself], the last novel to be discussed, is a fitting conclusion to this study, as it incorporates all the themes and settings of the previous novels, taking one more step forward in experience and broader horizons. Again, much of the personal life of Lera is discernible in this novel, paralleled by the story of Spain itself emerging from the Civil War, through the dictatorship of Franco, and on toward more freedom. The conclusion of this novel is open-ended, implying the beginning of a new cycle and hope for growth, and the reader catches the enthusiasm of an individual as well as a nation entering into maturity, self-awareness, and direction.

This is a confessional narrative told at first by the central figure, Enrique Lorca, a man of forty (corresponding to the age of Lera at the time of his release from prison). Seated in front of a barbershop mirror, symbolic of the painful journey to the limits of one's self, he gradually unfolds his past life to the barber. The latter, his older alter-ego, related to the later appearance of Lera himself in the novel, is appropriately named Victoriano because of his victory over himself. His philosophy, and that of the author, is the following:

Men are not masters of themselves. They are always chained to something. Even those who appear to be good and act like it, have other motives, just as the bad people act bad because they like to and because they want to be feared. It is more comfortable to be good, there's no doubt about that. But there are many times when the good person would like to be bad, but he doesn't dare to because it would mean a great effort and he would lose the fame which is so important for him to conserve. And the same thing happens with the bad people, who are tired of always going against the grain, confronting everything, but who have no other choice than to continue that way if they don't want to lose the upper hand and have people laugh at them. And note this: at times the good people drag us into insanity and to disaster, while the bad people bring good to men by obliging them to oppose their evil. Against pride one must bring humility, against anger, patience, etc. The good person who believes that he is good is as unbearable as he who does wrong. For me, virtue consists in making oneself bearable. In bearing with one another, having compassion for one another, and helping one another. (111)

Only later do we learn that this is a prison barbershop, a similar confessional technique found in Ernesto Sábato's *El túnel* [The Tunnel], Camilo José Cela's *La familia de Pascual Duarte* [The Family of Pascual Duarte], and Albert Camus's *L'étranger* [The Stranger]. Structured in nine chapters, the first five employ the above-mentioned technique with flashbacks to the past of Enrique and by extension, to the political, economic, and social atmosphere of contemporary Spain between 1936–1976.[1] It is the story of a single individual given over to a lucid acceptance of his times, allowing a nation's anguish to become his own. In a very real sense, he is the times, accepting within himself the rich and conflicting currents of an era of change.

Enrique's earliest childhood memories of an Andalusian village coincide with the Spanish Civil War (1936–1939) and are a surrealistic composite of recurring nightmares and his mother's accounts of those years. The most salient memory was the execution of his father in the cemetery at night by an anonymous firing squad, a poetic note that, because of his name, is obviously taken from the life of Federico García Lorca.[2] Enrique's ignorance as to whether his father was a Republican or a Fascist underscores the author's desire for neutrality, emphasizing the common tragedy of the war for all Spaniards. Later there followed bare survival by scavenging, the death of his younger sister from malnutrition, and his eventual journey to the capital with his mother.

Chapter 2 pictures their life in Madrid when Enrique was age ten to twelve, corresponding to the postwar period of Spain seen through the eyes of a young woman in Carmen Laforet's novel entitled *Nada* [Nothing]. It is a modern picaresque milieu with Enrique, the rebel, as a latter-day Oliver Twist facing a fragmented universe. The action centers around the Market of Legazpi in Madrid, with its organized gangs of young hoodlums (to which Enrique belongs), and the black-market negotiations. The setting is that of *The Forgotten Ones,* and again the main themes are the law of the jungle and hunger: "One single desire prevailed above all the rest, to eat, and one preoccupation above all the rest, to find food wherever it might be and at whatever cost" (35).[3] Yet there are notes of compassion and even humor (not found in *The Forgotten Ones*) as Enrique comes to know good from evil. Symbolically, at age twelve (the age of puberty), he defends his mother from a would-be attacker fittingly named Don Saturio and comments: "From that day Don Saturio didn't try to bother my mother and on that day also ended my childhood" (62).

In Chapter 3 of this apprenticeship novel Enrique, at age fourteen, abandons his dishonor and weapons for self-respect and his first job, voicing the title theme: "And so they sold me for the first time" (68). He works in a grocery store run by Señor Plácido, whose motto is: "He who doesn't cheat, doesn't beat." Quickly disillusioned by the slippery-fingered techniques of his boss, Enrique also makes other comments about the graft and corruption in postwar Spain. He focuses on the impoverished nobility who, like Lazaro's master in the sixteenth-century picaresque Spanish novel, *Lazarillo de Tormes,* refuse to give up appearances of wealth.

Emphasizing the underlying feelings of discontentment and even despair in postwar Spain, he says: "They are people with no other preoccupation than survival, with uncertainty on the horizon, oscillating continually between fear and anger. . . . I began to be aware of the infinite bonfires of hate that burn in their hearts, of the dusky sadness that is hidden behind the brightness of their smiles, of the frustrations and failures that are covered by the aggressive expression, of the dissatisfaction, the discontent and the rebellion that boil under the appearances of docility and conformity, and that there are very few persons that don't feel intimately misunderstood and imprisoned" (81). These images echo the fear and frustration of Rafa and Aceituno in *The Horns of Fear*; those who are uprooted and struggling to survive under poor economic conditions. This period coincides with that of postwar Spain and Lera's own precarious financial situation at the time.

Chapter 4 deals with Enrique's relationship with women. True to the Spanish mentality, he is very close to his mother, whom he reveres, and is greatly saddened by her death. At this time, however, he meets Maribel, whose name again reflects the Virgin-like quality associated with women, and whom he describes thus: "Her eyes were brilliant blue, serene and melancholy, in a face with small features . . . although a few years younger than myself, she appeared, nevertheless, an adolescent recently opened to the light. She was twenty years old and looked fifteen. Maribel was a slender girl, with temperate lines, like a boy. . . . Her hair was light brown with flecks of gold which she combed upward, leaving revealed her delicate neck and small ears" (91). Portrayed as both sinner and saint, Maribel is also the mistress of an older rich man. And Enrique not only suffers guilt because of his first sexual experience but is also disillusioned because he cannot marry her. Yet he matures with the experience, and, if he loses his initial romantic illusions about love, he is compensated because for the first time he feels "intimations of immortality" and learns to know himself through intimacy with another. He says: "I would like to know what dreams are, where we are going, and that night I felt curiosity of these things for the first time. . . . I found out then what a woman is, that she is much more than I had imagined, and also much less. That is to say, something completely different. Now I understand myself" (101). Discovering, albeit painfully, the deeper meaning of love, he continually reiterates the necessity for telling the truth, and, by extension, that Truth and Love must go hand in hand. "To lie is, in my judgment, to deny oneself. Not like Saint Peter denied Christ, but much worse, as if Christ had said to Pontius Pilate that he was not himself, the Christ, but rather a crazy man, an idiot, an innocent one. I continue to believe that lying is the worst vice and the greatest cowardice of man" (117).

Chapter 5 portrays a double step toward maturity as Enrique joins the military and learns the mechanic's trade. In the military he acquires self-discipline and broadens his world-view. He also finds time to read—in particular, the poetry of Federico García Lorca and biographies of Napoleon Bonaparte. But as he remarks: "Mechanics and traveling are what I have always dreamed about." Thus he sells himself for the second time, becoming a driver for his commanding officer, Pepe Migas (the name has the connotation of good friend or companion). Pepe is a Marxist and Enrique an Anarchist. The former, working under cover in Franco Spain, defends his position, saying: "One must do something. I expose myself to danger because it is the only thing I can do. If each of us would put in our grain of sand . . ." (150). Enrique, the Anarchist, fights to be himself, affirming that each

man must first learn to conquer himself, and soon wins the respect of
the older man. Friendship wins out over politics, a condition which the
author views as essential for the unity of Spain.[4] The remainder of the
chapter is an extension of the metaphor "Life is a road," reiterating the
prologue poem by Antonio Machado and the existential position of the
author. ("Everything changes and everything remains/but our task is
to walk,/to walk making our own roads,/roads over the sea.") In
true rolling-stone fashion, Enrique meets and learns from other women
and experiences, but there is no real emotional involvement or
commitment, and he has not put down roots.

Chapter 6 arrives at the present and we discover for the first time that
he has been in prison for six years. This is his fortieth birthday and also
the day of his release, the reclaiming of his birthright. His description
of the prison is similar to that in *We Who Lost,* but the latter is more
autobiographical in nature and related to the Civil War era. Here in this
chapter he makes reference to prison conditions under the dictatorship
in later years, and indeed Lera was again imprisoned in Madrid for a
brief period for underground political activities (described in *Dark
Dawn*). He refers to two groups: the political prisoners and the seasoned
criminals. The former intimidate him and the latter horrify him, so as a
result he becomes a loner. Sustained only by thoughts of revenge, he
begins Chapter 7 by stating: "I have paid what I did not owe, that is the
truth, and my only intention upon leaving jail consists in recovering
that debt" (189). His ride in a train after release from prison enables
him, by means of reverie, to reveal the cause of his imprisonment. After
leaving Pepe Migas he became a taxi-driver in Madrid, a position he
describes as a secular confessional from which to view the "Vanity Fair"
of the city. In keeping with this theme, Victoriano the barber
comments: "Life is a fair in which everyone buys and sells and in which
everything is bought and sold" (195). Here our Bunyan's pilgrim meets
José and Gloria Puig. José is the modern devil—glittering,
ambiguous, and charming—the big businessman involved in
construction.[5] For the third time Enrique sells himself, and when the
bottom falls out of the business, he is the scapegoat who is sent to
prison.

Continuing the above story, Chapter 8 is a mini-drama and mystery
story primarily played out in the mind and imagination of Enrique.
Ruminating over his planned revenge, he melodramatically imagines

himself holding a gun and boldly confronting José Puig. First comes the "macho" murder and then the passionate possession of Gloria, Jose's seductive wife. While waiting to gather up his courage, he passes through other monuments of modern society—the University of Madrid and the Prado Museum. This technique enables the author to vent some of his anti-intellectual antipathies and to affirm the worth of the individual in the face of society's great institutions. (It is also perhaps a reflection of his envy and frustration at not having been able to develop his own professional talents.)[6] Failing in his attempt to build up sufficient hatred for this task, Enrique throws his gun into a ditch, and the actual encounter is an anticlimax betraying the disparity between fantasy and reality, between the world of ideas and the world of form, which is the main theme of the chapter. In a conversation centering around the inhumanity of big business, Puig laments to Enrique that "The business owns me, I don't have time for anything. The monster. She is the one who doesn't have heart or conscience" (252). Enrique longs to respond that man is real and the business is a fiction, and that business ought to serve man and not the contrary. But he senses that it would fall on deaf ears and he leaves, saddened, but content with having conquered the violence and hatred within himself.

The past now behind him, Enrique goes on to meet his Master or Teacher in the form of the author, Lera himself, who as artist and creator supplants the role previously played by Victoriano. It is a technique used by Miguel de Unamuno in his novel *Niebla* [Mist], but here the protagonist is given free will by his "creator," who refuses to predestine or manipulate his characters. Lera, as in real life, is spending the summer at the sea in the small village of Aguilas. Their encounter occurs during the author's early-morning swim, described as a form of meditation and unity with the universe. In the ensuing dialogue between the two, the intensity and brevity of the questions reflect the earnestness of the questioner, recalling the figures of Mario and Miguel in *The Trap* and *Summer Storm*.

Question: Why do you write?
Answer: For the same reason that I live, although I know that I have to die.
Question: Are you satisfied?

Answer: No, never, after each failure, we repeat the adventure over and
            over again, in the same way that each day we try to live the life
            that we want to live. Because of that, writing is like living.

Question: You mean to say that life has no meaning, right?

Answer: The meaning which others try to give us, I doubt it. On the
            other hand the life that *we* desire, yes I believe that it has
            meaning. Because of that we live.

Question: Is complete liberty possible?

Answer: Both complete liberty and complete life are two unrealizable
            aspirations. In spite of that, it is necessary to fight till the end
            for both the one and the other if we want to be like gods.

Question: Can we live alone?

Answer: No, we cannot live unto ourselves because we only know ourselves
            and complete ourselves through others.

After the departure of his new disciple, the author/creator analyzes
his young friend's condition: "Enrique Lorca was, without a doubt, an
intelligent man, gifted with a great sensibility, introverted, sincere,
with a fragmentary culture and obsessed by a scrupulous demand for
authenticity. His story showed me that he had suffered many painful
deceptions in life and that because of that he distrusted men, he feared
them and, when possible, fled from them. Otherwise he interposed
between himself and others an inviolable dividing line. Was he an
egotist and coward, as he described himself? I would rather say that he
was a skeptic, and as a consequence, incapable of committing himself to
anything or anyone without a test. Closed within himself, but, at the
same time desirous of finding a convincing reason to come out of his
isolation. He was the opposite of a fanatic, in summary, he was an
idealist without an ideal" (266).

Lera becomes vitally interested in Enrique's case because of his belief
that man is master of his fate and his desire to see him conquer those
forces that seek to destroy him. Thus he carefully rewrites Enrique's
story from notes he had taken during their talks. Unable, however, to
finish the life story, he is suddenly aided by a letter from Enrique that
was sent from Munich. The contents provide a summary of his last two
years spent abroad since meeting the author and are reflective of Spain's
encounter with the two most influential nations on postwar Spanish
society: Germany and the United States. While at the beach, Enrique

had met Heidi, a German woman of twenty-eight with a ten-year-old son. He returned to Hamburg with them, working in her father's store. Like the Spanish emigrants who went to Germany to work, he was happy with the working conditions and the large salaries, but missed his homeland and was reluctant to commit himself. He therefore joined with a group of American hippies, believing them to represent perfect freedom. In particular, he is attached to a young woman named Jenny, from Oklahoma. But she is immature and he gradually learns to abhor the freedom without responsibility that she represents. Eventually he gets into a fight with a large black man and ends up in the hospital, where he has a chance to reflect.

Enrique, like Spain, realizes that he cannot imitate another culture and must seek to find his own identity. Thus he writes to Lera:

> I have lost no less than forty-two years—well, perhaps not completely lost because knowledge takes time, but at any rate, they were misspent years. More concretely, life is as it is and in order to live it one must fight for it and not let it slip through one's fingers like water. . . . Now that I am a man reborn, so to speak, and without a name yet, do you know what I am going to do when I leave the hospital? I am going to walk through the city with a sign on my back that says "Man for sale." Yes, "Man for sale," until someone comes to me with an offer of high human value, and perhaps I will succeed in giving meaning to my life. And do you know? I am afraid to commit myself, but I say to myself: Go on Enrique, it is the last chance to be a man, man, and free, free, free, like a god. (288)

In conclusion, the maturation of Enrique Lorca is that of Spain itself as it emerges from the Civil War, suffering the difficulties of postwar depression and oppression under the Franco regime. As Janet W. Díaz notes: "Posing the question whether the preservation of personal honesty and dignity are possible in such a context, the novel is a realistic and eloquent document of some of contemporary Spain's most difficult years. Ideologically simplistic, it is at the same time one further token of Lera's sincere devotion to the cause of social reform."[7] The weakness of the novel lays in its ideology, which, because of its very humanism, leaves one feeling that Enrique Lorca has still not found the ideal for which he is willing to make a commitment. The conclusion implies just one more "selling of himself," with the previous frustrations of not having found himself on firm footing. Written in 1973, the novel portrays a Spain unsure, like Enrique, as to where its future might lie. But the new direction being taken after an epoch of excess and despair satisfied a yearning for a freer, more meaningful, and more humanly acceptable existence. It is noteworthy that, after the public success of this novel, Lera went on to complete and publish his Civil War tetralogy. By the year 1978 Spain had witnessed the death of Franco and the restoration of the monarchy under Juan Carlos. Lera's biography of Angel Pestaña, written in that year, perceives the need of the nation for new models, new leaders, and a new identity. Thus he holds up as a possible example a man with great inner integrity and freedom.

Chapter 2 pictures their life in Madrid when Enrique was age ten to twelve, corresponding to the postwar period of Spain seen through the eyes of a young woman in Carmen Laforet's novel entitled *Nada* [Nothing]. It is a modern picaresque milieu with Enrique, the rebel, as a latter-day Oliver Twist facing a fragmented universe. The action centers around the Market of Legazpi in Madrid, with its organized gangs of young hoodlums (to which Enrique belongs), and the black-market negotiations. The setting is that of *The Forgotten Ones,* and again the main themes are the law of the jungle and hunger: "One single desire prevailed above all the rest, to eat, and one preoccupation above all the rest, to find food wherever it might be and at whatever cost" (35).[3] Yet there are notes of compassion and even humor (not found in *The Forgotten Ones*) as Enrique comes to know good from evil. Symbolically, at age twelve (the age of puberty), he defends his mother from a would-be attacker fittingly named Don Saturio and comments: "From that day Don Saturio didn't try to bother my mother and on that day also ended my childhood" (62).

In Chapter 3 of this apprenticeship novel Enrique, at age fourteen, abandons his dishonor and weapons for self-respect and his first job, voicing the title theme: "And so they sold me for the first time" (68). He works in a grocery store run by Señor Plácido, whose motto is: "He who doesn't cheat, doesn't beat." Quickly disillusioned by the slippery-fingered techniques of his boss, Enrique also makes other comments about the graft and corruption in postwar Spain. He focuses on the impoverished nobility who, like Lazaro's master in the sixteenth-century picaresque Spanish novel, *Lazarillo de Tormes,* refuse to give up appearances of wealth.

Emphasizing the underlying feelings of discontentment and even despair in postwar Spain, he says: "They are people with no other preoccupation than survival, with uncertainty on the horizon, oscillating continually between fear and anger. . . . I began to be aware of the infinite bonfires of hate that burn in their hearts, of the dusky sadness that is hidden behind the brightness of their smiles, of the frustrations and failures that are covered by the aggressive expression, of the dissatisfaction, the discontent and the rebellion that boil under the appearances of docility and conformity, and that there are very few persons that don't feel intimately misunderstood and imprisoned" (81). These images echo the fear and frustration of Rafa and Aceituno in *The Horns of Fear*; those who are uprooted and struggling to survive under poor economic conditions. This period coincides with that of postwar Spain and Lera's own precarious financial situation at the time.

Chapter 4 deals with Enrique's relationship with women. True to the Spanish mentality, he is very close to his mother, whom he reveres, and is greatly saddened by her death. At this time, however, he meets Maribel, whose name again reflects the Virgin-like quality associated with women, and whom he describes thus: "Her eyes were brilliant blue, serene and melancholy, in a face with small features . . . although a few years younger than myself, she appeared, nevertheless, an adolescent recently opened to the light. She was twenty years old and looked fifteen. Maribel was a slender girl, with temperate lines, like a boy. . . . Her hair was light brown with flecks of gold which she combed upward, leaving revealed her delicate neck and small ears" (91). Portrayed as both sinner and saint, Maribel is also the mistress of an older rich man. And Enrique not only suffers guilt because of his first sexual experience but is also disillusioned because he cannot marry her. Yet he matures with the experience, and, if he loses his initial romantic illusions about love, he is compensated because for the first time he feels "intimations of immortality" and learns to know himself through intimacy with another. He says: "I would like to know what dreams are, where we are going, and that night I felt curiosity of these things for the first time. . . . I found out then what a woman is, that she is much more than I had imagined, and also much less. That is to say, something completely different. Now I understand myself" (101). Discovering, albeit painfully, the deeper meaning of love, he continually reiterates the necessity for telling the truth, and, by extension, that Truth and Love must go hand in hand. "To lie is, in my judgment, to deny oneself. Not like Saint Peter denied Christ, but much worse, as if Christ had said to Pontius Pilate that he was not himself, the Christ, but rather a crazy man, an idiot, an innocent one. I continue to believe that lying is the worst vice and the greatest cowardice of man" (117).

Chapter 5 portrays a double step toward maturity as Enrique joins the military and learns the mechanic's trade. In the military he acquires self-discipline and broadens his world-view. He also finds time to read—in particular, the poetry of Federico García Lorca and biographies of Napoleon Bonaparte. But as he remarks: "Mechanics and traveling are what I have always dreamed about." Thus he sells himself for the second time, becoming a driver for his commanding officer, Pepe Migas (the name has the connotation of good friend or companion). Pepe is a Marxist and Enrique an Anarchist. The former, working under cover in Franco Spain, defends his position, saying: "One must do something. I expose myself to danger because it is the only thing I can do. If each of us would put in our grain of sand . . ." (150). Enrique, the Anarchist, fights to be himself, affirming that each man must first learn to conquer himself, and soon wins the respect of the older man. Friendship wins out over politics, a condition which the author views as essential for the unity of Spain.[4] The remainder of the chapter is an extension of the metaphor "Life is a road," reiterating the prologue poem by Antonio Machado and the existential position of the author. ("Everything changes and everything remains/but our task is to walk,/to walk making our own roads,/roads over the sea.") In true rolling-stone fashion, Enrique meets and learns from other women and experiences, but there is no real emotional involvement or commitment, and he has not put down roots.

Chapter 6 arrives at the present and we discover for the first time that he has been in prison for six years. This is his fortieth birthday and also the day of his release, the reclaiming of his birthright. His description of the prison is similar to that in *We Who Lost,* but the latter is more autobiographical in nature and related to the Civil War era. Here in this chapter he makes reference to prison conditions under the dictatorship in later years, and indeed Lera was again imprisoned in Madrid for a brief period for underground political activities (described in *Dark*

Dawn). He refers to two groups: the political prisoners and the seasoned criminals. The former intimidate him and the latter horrify him, so as a result he becomes a loner. Sustained only by thoughts of revenge, he begins Chapter 7 by stating: "I have paid what I did not owe, that is the truth, and my only intention upon leaving jail consists in recovering that debt" (189). His ride in a train after release from prison enables him, by means of reverie, to reveal the cause of his imprisonment. After leaving Pepe Migas he became a taxi-driver in Madrid, a position he describes as a secular confessional from which to view the "Vanity Fair" of the city. In keeping with this theme, Victoriano the barber comments: "Life is a fair in which everyone buys and sells and in which everything is bought and sold" (195). Here our Bunyan's pilgrim meets José and Gloria Puig. José is the modern devil—glittering, ambiguous, and charming—the big businessman involved in construction.[5] For the third time Enrique sells himself, and when the bottom falls out of the business, he is the scapegoat who is sent to prison.

Continuing the above story, chapter 8 is a mini-drama and mystery story primarily played out in the mind and imagination of Enrique. Ruminating over his planned revenge, he melodramatically imagines himself holding a gun and boldly confronting José Puig. First comes the "macho" murder and then the passionate possession of Gloria, Jose's seductive wife. While waiting to gather up his courage, he passes through other monuments of modern society—the University of Madrid and the Prado Museum. This technique enables the author to vent some of his anti-intellectual antipathies and to affirm he worth of the individual in the face of society's great institutions. (It is also perhaps a reflection of his envy and frustration at not having been able to develop his own professional talents.)[6] Failing in his attempt to build up sufficient hatred for this task, Enrique throws his gun into a ditch, and the actual encounter is an anticlimax betraying the disparity between fantasy and reality, between the world of ideas and the world of form, which is the main theme of the chapter. In a conversation centering around the inhumanity of big business, Puig laments to Enrique that "The business owns me, I don't have time for anything. The monster. She is the one who doesn't have heart or conscience" (252). Enrique longs to respond that man is real and the business is a fiction, and that business ought to serve man and not the contrary. But he senses that it would fall on deaf ears and he leaves, saddened, but content with having conquered the violence and hatred within himself.

Chapter Nine
Conclusion

The times in which Lera has been living and writing have been difficult ones, both for himself and Spain. The strife of civil war and the repression under a dictator and a struggle for survival were a heavy burden to bear. The author is to be forgiven if he seems too overly pessimistic, particularly in the war novels, and to view himself and others like him as "martyrs." His greatest strength has been his humanity; his ability to identify with the suffering of others and to seek solutions for social injustice. His ability to compromise has left him open to criticism, from both the left and the right. Yet his "middle-of-the-road" stance has in itself been a stand, a sometimes difficult one. From this position he has been able to integrate diverse interests and commitments and to further the cause of peace. His moral courage was manifest in his decision to stay in Spain and write, often under criticism and suppression. His boldness in determining to live by his pen and his unselfishness in devoting time to others have not detracted from the quality or intensity of his work.

Lera's concern for materialism, abuses by the clergy, political corruption, the plight of women, and educational stagnation—to mention only a few—have been paralleled by changes in society, albeit gradual. His nonfiction works dealing with the problems of emigration and rural medicine have also borne fruit in current awareness and reform. Whether Lera himself is in any way responsible for these changes is an open question. There is no doubt, however, of the authenticity of the man and the situations described in his novels.

Slowly but surely, and with self-discipline, he has succeeded in expressing publicly his humanitarian concerns and broad experiences. Always a good storyteller, his novels have had wide popular appeal, both at home and abroad. Furthermore, his writings manifest a steady growth and maturity, both with regard to style and content. His greatest literary fame will most likely rest with the civil-war tetralogy

The Years of Ire, and his earlier *The Horn of Fear.* In both these works his solution of a romantic realism both in life and art is appropriate, appropriate to his position within the mainstream of Spanish tradition and appropriate for one who survived the Spanish holocaust with his soul intact.

Future historians will judge his ultimate worth to Spanish letters. This current generation can be indebted to him for a life bravely lived, sometimes bitter, often beautiful, and a total involvement with the times. The contribution to date of his life and art includes a lucid understanding of the past (particularly the Spanish Civil War), a willingness to live generously in the present, and a sometimes prophetic vision of the future. Spain itself has emerged almost miraculously from the Franco era, seeking its identity in the modern world and hoping to better itself politically and economically. Lera describes this period well, revealing the strength of the Spaniards themselves, who have given an admirable example of maturity and serenity during these difficult times of the transition. Their recent decision to back King Juan Carlos and Prime Minister Suarez, and their ability to form a constitution is, in a sense, a realized dream. Lera's efforts and novels, along with those of many others, helped to sustain hope and pointed to solutions aimed at realizing this dream. Certainly the people will need time to become more aware and more involved in the political life of the country. But the foundation has been laid, and that foundation seems to be the beginning of better things to come.

Lera's latest work of nonfiction, *Angel Pestaña,* suggests the need for effective leadership for the future. And he himself continues to write, searching for truths, determined to fulfill his destiny. As Antonio Heras comments in his biography of the author: "You want to capture the life of a man is a few pages of a book, but you see that he escapes you like water through your fingers. You try to catch hold of the personality, the vital experiences, the thoughts of the man, but you only scratch the surface. It is then when you fully realize the greatness of a life, of the infinite cosmos that each human being carries within himself."[1]

Notes and References

Preface

1. The Premio Planeta, awarded by the Editorial Planeta, carries an award of more than 1,100,000 pesetas—the highest figure for a literary prize in Spain. This fact and the undoubted prestige conferred on the winner makes the Planeta a most sought-after award.

2. From December 1967 to February 1972, twenty editions of *Las últimas banderas* were published, with a total of 162,600 copies. This constituted, in effect, one of the greatest best-sellers in Spanish literature.

3. Angel María de Lera, *Los clarines de miedo,* ed. Robert Hatton (New York: Ginn, 1971).

4. Mary Sue Listerman, "The Narrative Art of Angel María de Lera," University of Missouri at Columbia (May 1963).

5. Another dissertation in progress is that of Owen Thomas, "Angel Maria de Lera: the Man and His Novel," New York University. See *Hispania* 60 (May 1977).

Chapter One

1. Angel María, Máximo, Jesús, Miguel Angel; Adelaida, Celia, María Guillermina, Angeles. Three children died early of pneumonia.

2. Luis Escolar Bareno, "Prólogo," *Novelas* by Angel María de Lera (Madrid, 1965), pp. ix–x. This and subsequent translations are mine.

3. *Angel Pestaña (Retrato de un anarquista)* (Barcelona, 1978).

4. See Antonio Beneyto, *Censura y política en los escritores españoles* (Madrid, 1975). Jaime Ferrán and Daniel Testa, *Spanish Writers of 1936* (London: 1973). Manuel Lamana, *Literatura de posguerra* (Mexico, 1971).

5. Eduardo de Guzman, "Prólogo," *Los fanáticos* by Angel María de Lera (Barcelona, 1969), p. 5.

6. Ibid., p. 10.

7. Antonio R. de las Heras, *Angel María de Lera* (Madrid, 1971), p. 62.

8. Frank Sedwick, "Angel de Lera: A Personal Note," *Los clarines del miedo,* ed. Robert Hatton (New York, 1971), p. xx.

9. Comments of Lera to the author in a series of interviews given in Madrid during June 1972. Subsequent comments included in this volume are from the same series of interviews.

10. Ramón de Garciasol, "Prólogo," *Angel María de Lera* by Antonio R. de las Heras, p. 6.

11. Comments of Lera to the author.

12. José Ramón Marra-López, "Diálogo con Angel María de Lera," *Insula* 16 (February 1961):4.

Chapter Two

1. José Ramón Marra-López, "Novela, relatos," *Insula* 174 (May 1961):8.

2. Eugenio Nora, *La novela española contemporánea (1898–1960)* (Madrid, 1962), p. 224.

3. Ibid., pp. 210, 289.

4. "The Spanish Novel: The Two Generations of the Civil War," *Spain Today* 3 (May 1970):30.

5. "La novela española, quince años después," *Cuadernos del Congreso por la Libertad de la Cultura* 33 (November–December 1958):51.

6. Pablo Gil Casado, *La novela social española* (Barcelona: Editorial Seix Barral, 1968), p. xvii.

7. Comments of Lera to the author.

8. Luis Ponce de León, "Más allá de las portadas," *Estafeta Literaria* 341 (April 9, 1966):15.

9. Ibid.

10. Antonio R. de las Heras, *Angel María de Lera,* p. 79.

11. Rollo May, *Love and Will* (New York: Norton, 1969), p. 272.

12. "[A substratum] in all the narrations of Lera is the sexual dissatisfaction of the Spaniards, the twisted and morbid sexuality that leads to crime and vaudeville." Antonio Iglesias Laguna, *Treinta años de la novela española (1938–1968)* (Madrid, 1969), p. 166.

13. Brenda Frazier, *La mujer en el teatro de Federico García Lorca* (Madrid: Playor, 1973), p. 232.

14. Manuel García Viño, "Última hora de la novela española," *Nuestro Tiempo* 137 (November 1965):481.

15. Comments of Lera to the author.

16. José María de Quinto, "*Los clarines del miedo,*" *Cuadernos Hispanoamericanos* 38 (April 1959):187.

17. In September 1975 I spoke with Dr. Ulrich Littman and his wife from Bonn, Germany. (He is the executive director of the Commission for Educational Exchange between the United States and Germany. This is a Fulbright Commission.) Both spoke of their concern for the foreign workers in Germany and of their personal efforts, as well as those of the German Government on their behalf (particularly the Spaniards).

A very successful monthly periodical, published in Spain but written for Spaniards living abroad, is entitled *Carta de España de emigración.*

18. Comments of Lera to the author.

19. "Prólogo," *Novelas,* p. xvi.

20. Paul Tillich, *The Eternal Now* (New York: Scribner, 1963), p. 122.

21. Angel María de Lera, *Los fanáticos* (Barcelona, 1969), p. 45.

22. "What great spirit his! What intellectual honesty and faithfulness to himself! I believe that the principal virtue of the writer, as of every real man after all is said and done, is authenticity." Angel María de Lera, *Por los caminos de la medicina rural* (Madrid, 1970), p. 35.

23. Pierre Teilhard de Chardin, *The Divine Milieu* (New York: Harper and Row, 1960).

24. Hera, p. 125, and comments of Lera to the author.

25. Ibid., p. 126.

26. "To be humble is a spiritual attitude, essentially intellectual and ethical. To be humble is to possess a clear awareness of the relativity of things and of values and a profound knowledge of life. Humility is the peak of wisdom." Angel María de Lera, *Los fanáticos,* p. 23.

27. John 4:24 (Revised Standard Version).

28. *Los fanáticos,* p. 14.

29. José Ramón Marra-López, "Diálogo con Angel María de Lera," *Insula* 171 (February 1961):4.

30. "Like Giovanni Verga's nineteenth century masterpiece, *The House by the Medlar Tree, The Wedding* builds its tragedy out of the simple materials of village life. . . . There is some Hemingway in the style and some Verga in both the use of setting and mood." Robert Spector, *New York Herald Tribune,* July 22, 1962, p. 7.

31. Heras, p. 135.

32. José Ramón Marra-López, p. 4.

33. José Luis Castillo-Puche, *Hemingway, entre la vida y la muerte* (Barcelona: Ediciones Destino, 1968), p. 467.

34. Angel María de Lera, "Prólogo," *Novelas,* p. xviii.

35. Comments of Lera to the author.

36. Heras, p. 83.

Chapter Three

1. Antonio R. de las Heras, *Angel María de Lera,* p. 111.

2. Idolized Communist leader in Spain who is discussed in detail later in this chapter.

3. Angel María de Lera, *Las últimas banderas* (Barcelona, 1967). This and subsequent quotations are from this edition.

4. Jean A. Schalekamp, "Novela antifalangista sobre la guerra civil premiada en Espana: *Las últimas banderas,*" *Norte* (Amsterdam), December 1967.

5. Angel María de Lera, *Los que perdimos* (Barcelona, 1974). This and subsequent quotations are from this edition.

6. John Donne, *Devotions,* ed. by John Sparrow (Cambridge, England, 1923), p. 98.

7. She is still living and returned to Spain from exile after the death of Franco.

8. Carmen Alcalde, *La mujer en la guerra civil española,* (Madrid: 1976), p. 209.

9. Albert Camus, *Alger-Républicain,* February 18, 1939, p. 5.

10. Angel María de Lera, *La noche sin riberas* (Barcelona, 1976). This and subsequent quotations are from this edition.

11. There are some similarities of title and theme with those found in *Dawn* by Elie Wiesel, translated from the French by Frances Frenage (New York: Hill and Wang, 1961).

12. Both novels deal with the Franco era, details of which can be verified by Max Gallo, *Spain Under Franco,* translated from the French by Jean Stewart (New York: Dutton, 1974).

13. Angel María de Lera, *Oscuro amanecer* (Barcelona, 1977). This and subsequent quotations are from this edition.

14. Elie Wiesel, "Art and Culture after the Holocaust," lecture presented at Miami University, March 4, 1978.

15. Gerald Green, "A Wreath on the Graves of Six Million," *TV Guide,* April 15, 1978, p. 8.

Chapter Four

1. I witnessed these slums, still present in 1963, although many were being improved by the government. They were similar to the more publicized *favelas* in Brazil.

2. Angel María de Lera, *Novelas* (Madrid, 1964). This and subsequent quotations from *Los olvidados* are from this edition.

3. "There are many and different ways in which a person can respond to an entrenched sense of fear and inadequacy. The response of the 'machista' is to resist it, to defy its depression and apathy, to go to the opposite extreme, to transcend the universally unbearable fear of aloneness and weakness through acting bigger, stronger, more glorious. . . . Many factors make up the 'machismo' complex, in a range that runs from climate to food and includes atavism, tradition, and problems that seem insurmountable; de-

structiveness in word and action; accompanied by high rates of homicide, general criminality, and alcoholism." Aniceto Aramoni, "Machismo," *Psychology Today,* January 1972, pp. 69–72.

4. Antonio R. de las Heras, *Angel María de Lera,* p. 51.

5. Ibid., pp. 51–52. "Antonio Pareja and Angel María de Lera knew each other in the Prison of Ocaña. Pareja was the figure of a pure anarchist who lives his anarchism as the most profound of religions. In the prison he demonstrated to Lera and to all his friends the firmness of his principle; his companion—as he called her—, appears in the novel with the name of Minerva, and by means of scrubbing floors was able to take Pestaña a can of condensed milk from time to time; he had a stomach ulcer. Nevertheless, the cans of milk disappeared, since he didn't drink them: he gave them, so that no one would find out, to others more needy. He died in the prison because of the ulcer."

6. Angel María de Lera, *Por los caminos de la medicina rural* (Madrid, 1969), p. 22.

7. Gÿorg Lúkacs, *The Theory of the Novel,* Tr. Anna Bostock (Cambridge, Mass.: M.I.T. Press, 1971).

8. José Ramón Marra-López, *"Los olvidados,"* *Insula* 16 (May 1961):8.

Chapter Five

1. José Ramón Marra-López, *"La boda,"* *Insula,* 10.

2. A reference to the lack of progress and social paralysis in Spain.

3. Rollo May, *Love and Will,* p. 272.

4. For a general study of the bullfight theme in literature see Miguel de Salabert, *Los toros en la literatura contemporánea* (Madrid, 1959).

5. Comments of Lera to the author.

6. Angel María de Lera, *Novelas* (Madrid, 1964). This and subsequent quotations from *Los clarines del miedo* are from this edition.

7. Comments of Lera in an interview following the publication of the novel, in *El Español,* June 1958, p. 222.

8. Antonio R. de las Heras, *Angel María de Lera,* p. 72.

9. José María Quinto, *"Los clarines del miedo,"* *Cuadernos Hispanoamericanos* 113 (May 1959):88.

10. "Se me falló la izquierda" is an idiom that means "to have lost courage." The British translation of the novel mistranslates literally ("my left arm failed me").

11. Antonio Iglesias Laguna, *Treinta años de novela española (1938–1968),* p. 166.

12. Considered by many to have been the greatest Spanish matador.

13. Manuel Benitez Pérez, Spain's foremost living matador. A "Rags to Riches" living legend with great charm and daring, he retired in 1972 but returned briefly to the arena in August 1979.

14. Title of an article by José M. Albertos, *Nuestro Tiempo,* September 1958, pp. 374–77.

15. "In Lera and others of his generation it is not easy to uncover a deep religiosity, but [it is] to collide with their Catholicism, which is invisibly installed in the innermost recesses of an apparent secularism." Gonzalo Sobejano, *Novela española de nuestro tiempo,* (Madrid, 1970), p. 207.

16. Federico Carlos Sáinz de Robles, *Madrid,* May 8, 1958.

17. Heras, p. 27.

18. Found in the collection entitled *Cuentos valencianos.*

19. The festival is in honor of Saint John the Baptist, and on that day every river is believed to carry a drop of the River Jordan, producing miracles. It is also related to the date of the summer solstice (June 21), and the festivities have vestiges of the pagan rites celebrating the advent of summer. The Greeks and Romans used to build bonfires in order to help the god of light to triumph over the god of darkness, and it is also considered a propitious time for lovers (as in Shakespeare's *A Midsummer Night's Dream*).

20. Angel María de Lera, *Novelas* (Madrid, 1964). This and subsequent quotations from *La boda* are from this edition.

21. A novel about an Italian Mafia family in America written by Mario Puzo (New York, 1969), which was made into a movie.

22. "When I strive to prove my potency in order to cover up and silence my inner fears of impotence, I am engaging in a pattern as ancient as man himself. Death is the symbol of ultimate impotence and finiteness, and anxiety arising from this inescapable experience calls forth the struggle to make ourselves infinite by way of sex. Sexual activity is the most ready way to silence the inner dread of death and, through the symbol of procreation, to triumph over it." Rollo May, *Love and Will,* p. 106.

23. Sigmund Freud, *The Ego and the Id,* trans. Joan Riviere (London: Hogarth Press, 1949), p. 47.

24. May, p. 149.

25. The word for "cock" in Spanish is *gallo.* And the dawn mass is called the *Misa de Gallo.*

26. During the years in prison, the only reading material available to Lera was a collection of works by Lope de Vega, a Spanish dramatist of the Golden Age. (Comments of Lera to the author.)

27. "The woman is a trophy in an arena disputed by men. It is reminiscent of Knighthood . . . but among 'machos' . . . the woman is a prize. As a person she matters little. Significantly, three women are spared this humiliation: sister, mother, and the Virgin. . . The Virgin is idolized, the

quintessence of a sublimated all-powerful mother. . . . The son belongs to the woman-mother faction, the feminine world; he is to betray the father, the masculine faction and himself. The mother holds him back from maturity, she creates in him powerful feelings of guilt and inferiority and, as these develop, anxiety joins them. . . . Other factors at work here are a religion that demands reverence for parents, and cultural elements that reward loyalty to parents and ostracize the disloyal." Aniceto Aramoni, "Machismo," *Psychology Today*, January 1972, p. 72.

Chapter Six

1. ". . . One cannot ask of life more than it can give, and it is that modest vial of illusion and hope which we find in our saddlebag at birth and from which we have to nourish ourselves all along the road that lies ahead of us. It is not wise, therefore, to use it up in a hurry, at one gulp, unless we want to soon perish from apathy and emptiness. The heroic recourse of escape, the flight in search of what we might call the fourth dimension of life usually ends up, in the best of cases, in a photograph like that of Heddy Lemar, who from portraying the role of Aphrodite . . . has come to be a sad news item in the newspaper. . . . She is empty inside, without wings, truly dead, and, what is even worse, without being able to find that rest, that human gravity, that she seems so desperately to need." Angel Maria de Lera, "La cuarta dimensión," *Los fanáticos* (Barcelona, 1969), p. 140.

2. Angel María de Lera, *Novelas* (Madrid, 1964). This and subsequent quotations from *Bochorno* are taken from this edition.

3. These and other problems of the educational system, with particular reference to the University of Madrid, are further enumerated in his newspaper article "La universidad, milagro," reproduced in *Los fanáticos,* pp. 219–23.

4. Antonio R. de las Heras, *Angel María de Lera,* p. 102.

5. "¿Revolución universitaria?" *Los fanáticos,* p. 111.

6. Angel María de Lera, *Novelas* (Madrid, 1964). This and subsequent quotations from *Trampa* are taken from this edition.

7. Heras, p. 102.

8. Ibid., p. 103.

9. Comments of Lera to the author.

Chapter Seven

1. Angel María de Lera, *Con la maleta al hombro* (Madrid, 1966). This nonfictional work is well documented with pictures and provides verification for the background material found in *Hemos perdido el sol.*

2. My husband worked for Klöckner-Deutz, a tractor factory in Cologne. He unloaded boxcars and worked on an assembly line with several Spaniards as well as other foreigners and Germans. There were some dormitory facilities available, but many workers had to find their own housing, often in lower class hotels and old tenement buildings. The food in the factory was ample if not appetizing, and the work area was efficient and clean, although the noise level was high. We were invited to the homes of several of the German overseers, one of them a former Nazi.

3. All Mediterranean peoples (Spaniards, Italians, Greeks) as well as Turks and Arabs were linked together as second-class citizens because of their position as *Gasterbeiters* ("guest workers") and their dark skins. It is true that there were conflicts among the workers themselves and that they sometimes were drunk and noisy on the streets. Many of them gathered at the large train station at night for lack of a meeting place or diversion, and we did witness more than several brawls and knife fights.

4. I attended German classes for foreigners taught by a German, Herr Mack, who had been tortured by the Nazis during World War II. I was inspired by his warmth, humor, and compassion toward his foreign students.

5. Angel María de Lera, *Hemos perdido el sol* (Madrid, 1963). This and subsequent quotations from *Hemos perdido el sol* are from this edition.

6. Comments of Lera to the author. As another example of German women, I cite the case of Frau Herring, a widow with whom my husband lived while a student in Cologne. Although he did pay for his room and board, she treated him, and later myself, as family. She helped us find an apartment, gave us the only dishes we had, and often invited us to her home to eat, offering us the best that she had. We returned several years later to visit her in the hospital as she lay dying of cancer. She was a brave and loving woman.

7. Antonio R. de las Heras, *Angel María de Lera,* p. 116.

8. William Shakespeare, *Macbeth,* act V, scene v, line 17.

9. Josuah led the Israelites into the Promised Land. Issac was to be sacrificed as a child by his father Abraham but was saved by God. Naomi was the mother-in-law of Ruth, who out of love, followed Naomi to her homeland when they were both widows.

10. Angel María de Lera, *Tierra para morir* (Madrid, 1966). This and subsequent quotations from *Tierra para morir* are from this edition.

11. John Donne, *Devotions,* ed. John Sparrow (Cambridge: At the University Press, 1923), p. 98. The title of Ernest Hemingway's novel *For Whom the Bell Tolls* is taken from this line.

Chapter Eight

1. I have consulted several authorities on contemporary Spain in order to verify the validity of the novel. Most helpful have been Stanley G. Payne, *Politics and the Military in Modern Spain* (Stanford, Calif.: Stanford University Press, 1967). Julián Lago, *La España transitiva* (Barcelona: 1976). A. Rivera Tovar, *La otra querra de la posquerra* (Madrid, 1968).

2. Federico García Lorca (1898–1936), universally renowned poet and dramatist who died tragically at the beginning of the Civil War. He was supposedly killed by a Fascist firing squad at Granada.

3. Angel María de Lera, *Se vende un hombre* (Barcelona, 1973). This and subsequent quotations are from this edition.

4. Comments of Lera to the author.

5. I witnessed such boom construction in Madrid in 1963 and in Andalucía in 1979. Many of the projects were abandoned because of lack of funds and others manifested severe inadequacies in material and construction.

6. Lera views each individual as a cosmos and recognizes within himself the talents of a teacher, a writer, a public speaker, a physician, etc. (comments of Lera to the author).

7. Janet W. Díaz, "Se vende un hombre," *Hispania* 58 (December 1975):969–70.

Chapter Nine

1. Heras, *Angel María de Lera,* p. 90.

Selected Bibliography

PRIMARY SOURCES

1. Fiction
Los olvidados. Colección Nova Navis. Madrid: Aguilar, 1957.
Los clarines del miedo. Colección Ancora y Delfin. Barcelona: Destino, 1958.
La boda. Collección Ancora y Delfin. Barcelona: Destino, 1959.
Bochorno. Colección Novela Nueva. Madrid: Aguilar, 1962.
Trampa. Colección Novela Nueva. Madrid: Aguilar, 1962.
Hemos perdido el sol. Colección Novela Nueva. Madrid: Aguilar, 1963.
Novelas. Prologue by Luis Escolar Bareño. Biblioteca de Autores Modernos.
    Madrid: Aguilar, 1965. (*Los olvidados, Los clarines del miedo, La Boda,*
    Bochorno and *Trampa.*)
Las últimas banderas. Barcelona: Planeta, 1967.
Tierra para morir. Colección Novela Nueva. Madrid: Aguilar, 1969.
Se vende un hombre. Barcelona: Planeta, 1973.
Los que perdimos. Barcelona: Planeta, 1974.
La noche sin riberas. Barcelona: Argos, 1976.
Oscuro Amanecer. Barcelona: Argos, 1977.

2. Nonfiction
Con la maleta al hombro. Madrid: Editorial Nacional, 1965.
Los fanáticos. Colección Rayo de Luz. Barcelona: Editorial Linosa, 1969.
Por los caminos de la medicina rural. Colección Testigos de España. Madrid:
    Plaza and Lanes, 1970.
Mi viaje alrededor de la locura. Barcelona: Planeta, 1972.
Angel Pestaña. (Biografía de un anarquista). Barcelona: Argos, 1978.

3. Articles in *ABC* (Madrid)
"Otro paraíso que se pierde." October 10, 1963, pp. 11–12.
"Juan Bosch, escritor y americano universal." May 4, 1967, pp. 22–23.
"Segrelles, ilustrador de *El Quijote.*" May 25, 1967, p. 13.
"Contamos contigo." June 1, 1967, p. 17.

"Un botón de muestra." June 8, 1967, p. 15.
"Libros que hay que tener." June 15, 1967, p. 17.
"¿Que es la sociedad de autores?" June 22, 1967, p. 19.
"Los trabajos de Américo Castro." August 24, 1967, p. 15.
"Américo Castro." December 19, 1968, p. 13.
"Cervantes en U.S.A.: el segundo idioma." May 22, 1969, p. 11.
"Cervantes en U.S.A.: el libro español aquí." June 5, 1969, pp. 10–11.
"Cervantes en U.S.A.: los profesores españoles." June 12, 1969, pp. 8–9.
"Bienvenidos a casa." June 26, 1969, p. 9.
"Crónicas de Canarias." August 7, 1969, p. 13.
"Buero Vallejo y la literatura de la posguerra." February 25, 1971, p. 13.

SECONDARY SOURCES

1. Books

Bosch, Rafael. *La novela española del siglo XX.* New York: Las Americas, 1971, 2:172–79, Vol II. Discusses *Bochorno, Trampa, Hemos perdido el sol,* and *Las últimas banderas.* Provides good introduction to the social and literary climate of the period between the Republic and the postwar period.

Calderón, E. Correa, and Carreter, F. Lázaro. *Literatura española contemporánea.* Salamanca: Anaya, 1963. Discusses *Los clarines del miedo,* giving it a place of prominence in Spanish letters as well as a unique example of taurine literature.

Corrales Egea, José. *La novela española actual.* Madrid: Edicusa, 1971, pp. 166–75. Praises *Los clarines del miedo* in a ten-page discussion that includes character analysis and theme development, as well as the social climate and background.

Díaz-Plaja, Guillermo. *La creación literaria en España.* Madrid: Aguilar, 1968. Discusses in some detail *Las últimas banderas,* pp. 366–69. Praises Lera for his objectivity and historical accuracy, while sympathizing with the Republican cause.

Domingo, José. *La novela española del siglo XX.* Barcelona: Editorial Labor, S.A., 1973, Vol. II. Discusses in some detail *Las últimas banderas,* pp. 28–29. Refers to other novels of the Civil War that treat of the same historical period, i.e. the last days of the war in Madrid, p. 90.

Gil Casado, Pablo. *La novela social española*. Barcelona: Editorial Seix Barral, 1968. Provides a bibliography including critical articles and ten pages of discussion over eight of Lera's novels.

Heras, Antonio R. de las. *Angel María de Lera*. Madrid: E.P.E.S.A., 1971, pp. 188-. Imaginative biography and literary criticism by one of Lera's journalism protégés. The pivotal point of departure is Lera's release from prison. His point of view is objective but colored by his admiration for the author, and his psychological insights are astute.

Iglesias Laguna, Antonio. *Treinta años de novela española. 1938–1969.* Madrid: Prensa Española, 1970. Makes numerous references to Lera and briefly discusses all of his works prior to 1970.

Nora, Eugenio de. *La novela española contemporánea*. Madrid: Gredos, 1962. Classifies Lera in several categories: traditional, writers living during the war, and postwar writers. Vol. III.

Sainz de Robles, Federico Carlos. *El espíritu y letra (Cien años de la literatura española: 1860–1960)*. Madrid: Aguilar, 1966, p. 219. Brief biography and bibliography up to *Con la maleta al hombro*.

Sobejano, Gonzalo. *Novela española de nuestro tiempo*. Madrid: Editorial Prensa Española, 1970, p. 207. Good discussion of the generation of Lera, helping to place him in context with the period.

Torrente Ballester, Gonzálo. *Panorama de la literatura española contemporánea*. Madrid: Ediciones Guadarrama, 1961, Vol. I (p. 432); Vol. II (pp. 777–81). Praises *Los clarines del miedo* and *La boda,* with a selection from the former novel used as an example of style. Critical of *Bochorno,* pointing out the author's lack of first-hand knowledge of the situation.

2. Articles

Bosch, Rafael. *"Hemos perdido el sol."* *Revista Hispánica Moderna* (New York) 3.

Cano, Jose Luis. *"Las últimas banderas."* *Insula* (Madrid), February 1969.

Dicenta de Vera, F. *"La boda."* *Las Provincias* (Valencia), June 30, 1959.

Fernández Almagro, Melchor. *"Trampa."* *ABC,* 1962.

Gallego, Gregorio. "La novela social española de Angel María de Lera." *Communidad Ibérica* (Mexico), October 1967.

Iglesias Laguna, Antonio. "Angel María de Lera, novelista de lo elmental." *El Español* (Madrid), June 1, 1968.

Miró, Emilio, "El último Planeta." *Estafeta Literaria* (Madrid), October 23, 1965.

Panero, Leopoldo. "Tragedias noveladas." *Blanco v negro* (Madrid), August 1, 1959.

Ponce de León, Luis. "El novelista Angel María de Lera." *Estafeta literaria* (Madrid), No. 391 (April 9, 1966).

Seannell, Vernon. "The Wedding." *Listener* (London), March 22, 1962.

Serrano, María Dolores. "Angel María de Lera: Premio gordo de las letras." *Gaceta Ilustrada* (Madrid), October 22, 1967.

Singer, Burns. *"The Horns of Fear." Listener* (London), April 6, 1961.

Tarn, John. *"The Horns of Fear." Books and Book Men* (London), June 1961.

Index